URBAN TRANSPORTATION PLANNING IN THE UNITED STATES

URBAN TRANSPORTATION PLANNING IN THE UNITED STATES

An Historical Overview

Edward Weiner

New York
Westport, Connecticut
London

Library of Congress Cataloging-in-Publication Data

Weiner, Edward.
  Urban transportation planning in the United States.

  Bibliography: p.
  1. Urban transportation policy – United States –
History. I. Title.
HE308.W45 1987   388.4′068   86–30343
ISBN 0-275-92493-9 (alk. paper)
ISBN 0-275-92544-7 (pbk. : alk. paper)

Library of Congress Catalog Card Number: 86–30343
ISBN: 0-275-92493-9
      0-275-92544-7 (pbk)

First published in 1987

Praeger Publishers, 521 Fifth Avenue, New York, NY 10175
A division of Greenwood Press, Inc.

Printed in the United States of America

∞

The paper used in this book complies with the Permanent
Paper Standard issued by the National Information Standards
Organization (Z39.48-1984).

10 9 8 7 6 5 4 3 2 1

to my children
Jennifer Lynn and Michael Andrew

CONTENTS

PREFACE

Recent evolution of the urban transportation planning function has placed greater emphasis on the role of state and local decision makers in the implementation of transportation system changes. In this context, it is important to understand the transportation and planning options that have been tried, and how they developed into the approaches we have today. This book describes the evolution of urban transportation planning over the last fifty years.

The book focuses on key events in the evolution of urban transportation planning including developments in technical procedures, philosophy, processes, and institutions. But planners must also be aware of changes in legislation, policy, regulations, and technology. These events have been included to provide a more complete picture of the forces that have affected and often continue to affect urban transportation planning.

This book is an updated version of "Evolution of urban transportation planning," which was published in 1979 as Chapter 15 in *Public Transportation: Planning, Operations and Management*, edited by George E. Gray and Lester L. Hoel (Englewood Cliffs, NJ: Prentice-Hall, 1979). The earlier version discussed urban transportation planning to mid 1976. This book updates the evolution of urban transportation planning and policy to the end of 1985. It also contains many additions and some revisions to the earlier edition.

A "Chronology of Significant Events" has been added in an Appendix. It was originally prepared as lecture notes to assist the author in describing the subject matter. It is hoped that this chronology will aid the reader in following the sometimes intricate web of events in this field.

Summarizing so much history in a short book requires difficult choices. The efforts of many individuals and groups made important contributions to the development of urban transportation planning. Clearly, not all of these contributions could be included or cited. This book concentrates on the key events of national significance and thereby tries to capture the overall evolution of urban transportation planning. Focusing on key events also serves as a convenient point to discuss developments in a particular area.

The book is generally arranged chronologically. Each period is titled with the major theme pervading that period as viewed by the author. Not all key events fit precisely under a particular theme, but many do. The discussion of the background for some events or the follow-on activities for others may cover more than one time period and is placed where it seemed most relevant.

Over the years, the author has discussed these events with many persons in the profession. Often they had participated in or had first hand knowledge of the events. The author appreciates their assistance, even though they are too numerous to mention specifically.

In preparing this book, the author was directly aided by several individuals who provided information on specific events. Their assistance is appreciated: Elizabeth A. Parker, Barry Berlin, Sam Rea, Thomas Koslowski, Norman Paulhus, James A. Scott, Norman Cooper, Camille C. Mittelholtz, Ira Laster, John Peak, and Carl Rappaport.

The author appreciates the review comments provided by: Donald Emerson, David S. Gendell, James Getzewich, Charles H. Graves, Thomas J. Hillegass, Howard S. Lapin, Alfonso B. Linhares, Gary E. Maring, Ali F. Sevin, Peter R. Stopher, Carl N. Swerdloff, and Paul L. Verchinski.

The author acknowledges the special contributions of Dr. Peter R. Stopher and Norman Paulhus for their encouragement and persistence throughout this project.

This book could not have been completed without the assistance of Joanne Kormos and Loretta Graham in the preparation of this manuscript, who always performed their work in a cheerful manner.

Any errors of fact or interpretation are the responsibility of the author.

1
INTRODUCTION

Almost twenty-five years have passed since the Federal Aid Highway Act of 1962 created the federal mandate for urban transportation planning in the United States. The act was the capstone of two decades of experimentation and development of urban transportation procedures and institutions. It was passed at a time in which urban areas were beginning to plan Interstate highway routes through and around their areas. The 1962 Act combined with the incentive of 90 percent federal funding for Interstate highway projects caused urban transportation planning to spread quickly throughout the United States. It also had a significant influence on urban transportation planning in other parts of the world.

In some ways, the urban transportation planning process and planning techniques have changed little over the twenty-five years. Yet, in other ways, urban transportation has evolved over these years in response to changing issues, conditions, and values, and a greater understanding of urban transportation phenomena. Current urban transportation planning practice is considerably more sophisticated, complex, and costly than its highway planning predecessor.

Modifications in the planning process took many years to evolve. As new concerns and issues arose, changes in planning techniques and processes were introduced. These modifications sought to make the planning process more responsive and sensitive to those areas of concern. Urban areas that had the resources and technical ability were the first to develop new concepts and techniques. These new ideas were diffused by various means throughout the nation, usually with the assistance of the federal government. The rate at which the new concepts were accepted varied from area to area. Consequently, the quality and depth of planning is highly variable at any point in time.

Early highway planning concentrated on developing a network of all-weather highways and with connecting the various portions of the nation. As this work was being accomplished, the problems of serving increasing traffic grew. With the planning for urban areas came additional problems of land development, dislocation of homes and businesses, environmental degradation, citizen participation, and social concerns such as providing transportation for the disadvantaged. More recently have been the concerns about energy consumption and deterioration of the transportation infrastructure.

Urban transportation planning in the United States has always been conducted by state and local agencies. This is entirely appropriate since highway and transit facilities and services are owned and operated largely by the states and local agencies. The role of the federal government has been to set national policy, provide financial aid, supply technical assistance and training, and conduct research. Over the years, the federal government has attached requirements to its financial assistance. From a planning perspective, the most important has been the requirement that transportation projects in urbanized areas of 50,000 or more in population be based on an urban transportation planning process. This requirement was first incorporated into the Federal Aid Highway Act of 1962.

Other requirements have been incorporated into federal legislation and regulations over the years. Many of these are chronicled in this report. At times these requirements have been very exacting in their detail. At other times, greater flexibility was allowed in responding to the requirements. Currently, there is underway a devolution of federal involvement in and requirements on local planning and decision making processes. Greater emphasis is being placed as well on involving the private sector in providing and financing urban transportation facilities and services.

Over the years, a number of federal agencies have affected urban transportation planning (Table 1.1). The U.S. Bureau of Public Roads was part of the U.S. Department of Commerce when the 1962 Highway Act was passed. It became part of the U.S. Department of Transportation (DOT) upon its creation in 1966 and its name changed to the U.S. Federal Highway Administration. The federal urban mass transportation program began in 1961 under the U.S. Hous-

TABLE 1.1. Founding Dates of Selected Federal Agencies

1916	Bureau of Public Roads
1921	Bureau of the Budget
1947	Housing and Home Finance Agency
1953	Department of Health, Education and Welfare
1965	Department of Housing and Urban Development
1966	Department of Transportation, and Federal Highway Administration
1968	Urban Mass Transportation Administration
1969	Council on Environmental Quality
1970	Office of Management and Budget, and Environmental Protection Agency
1977	Department of Energy
1979	Department of Health and Human Services

ing and Home Finance Administration, which became the U.S. Department of Housing and Urban Development in 1965. The federal urban transit program was transferred to DOT in 1968 as the U.S. Urban Mass Transportation Administration.

Other federal agencies became involved in urban transportation planning as new issues arose. The Bureau of the Budget, later to become the Office of Management and Budget, issued guidance in 1969 to improve coordination among programs funded by the federal government. To address environmental concerns that were increasing in the latter part of the 1960s, the Council on Environmental Quality was created in 1969 and the U.S. Environmental Protection Agency in 1970. The U.S. Department of Health, Education and Welfare became involved in urban transportation in 1973 as part of its function to eliminate discrimination against handicapped persons in federal programs. In 1977, the U.S. Department of Energy was created to bring together federal energy functions.

The involvement of these and other agencies at the federal, state, and local level created an increasing challenge to agencies conducting urban transportation planning to meet all the requirements that resulted. Local planners devoted substantial resources to meeting requirements of higher level governments, which often detracted from their ability to address local needs and objectives. These requirements, however, were also used by local agencies as the justification to carry out activities that they desired but for which they could not obtain support at the local level.

This report reviews the historical development of the urban transportation planning process in the United States from its beginnings in early highway and transit planning to the most recent focus on decentralization of decision making:

Chapter 2 discusses the early beginnings of highway planning.

Chapter 3 covers the formative years of urban transportation planning during which many of the basic concepts were developed.

Chapter 4 focuses on the 1962 Federal Aid Highway Act and the sweeping changes it brought in urban transportation planning in the United States. It also describes early federal involvement in urban public transportation.

Chapter 5 discusses efforts at intergovernmental coordination, a deeper federal role in urban public transportation and the evolution to ''continuing'' transportation planning.

Chapter 6 describes the environmental revolution of the late 1960s and the increased involvement of citizens in the urban transportation planning process.

Chapter 7 addresses the events that led to integrated planning for urban public transportation and highways. These included major increases in federal transit programs as well as increased flexibility in the use of highway funds.

Chapter 8 focuses on the Arab oil embargo of 1973, which accelerated the transition from long-term system planning to short-term, smaller scale planning. It also discusses the concern for cost-effectiveness in transportation decisions and the emphasis on transportation system management techniques.

Chapter 9 highlights the concern for the revitalization of older urban centers and the growing need for energy conservation. It describes the expanding federal requirements on environmental quality and transportation for special groups.

Chapter 10 describes the efforts to reverse federal intrusion into local decisions and to scale back federal requirements.

Chapter 11 discusses the growing interest in involving the private sector in the provision of transportation services.

Chapter 12 provides concluding remarks.

2
EARLY HIGHWAY PLANNING

Need for Highway Planning

In the early years of highway construction, the automobile had been regarded as a pleasure vehicle rather than an important means of transportation. Consequently, highways consisted of comparatively short sections that were built from the cities into the countryside. During this period, urban roads were considered to be adequate, particularly in comparison to rural roads. Although the concept of a continuous national system of highways was recognized in the Federal Aid Highway Act of 1925, there were significant gaps in many important intercity routes. In addition, highway pavements were largely inadequate to carry major traffic loads.

The need for a systematic approach to the planning of highways was recognized in the early 1930s as the rapid growth in automobile ownership and highway travel placed increasing demands on an inadequate highway system. It became clear that these growing problems necessitated the collection and analysis of information on highways and their use on a more comprehensive scale than had ever before been attempted (Holmes and Lynch, 1957).

Federal Aid Highway Act of 1934

Beginning with the Federal Aid Highway Act of 1934, the Congress authorized that 1.5 percent of the amount apportioned to any state annually for construction could be used for surveys, plans, engineering, and economic analyses for future highway construction projects. The act created the cooperative arrangement between the U.S. Bureau of Public Roads (now the U.S. Federal Highway Administration) and the state highway departments, known as the statewide highway planning surveys. By 1940, all states were participating in this program (Holmes and Lynch, 1957).

As an initial activity, these highway planning surveys included a complete inventory and mapping of the highway system and its physical characteristics. Traffic surveys were undertaken to determine the volume of traffic by vehicle type, weight, and dimensions. Financial studies were made to determine the relationship of highway finances to other financial operations within each state, to assess the ability of the states to finance the construction and operation of the highway system, and to indicate how to allocate highway taxes among the users. Many of the same types of activities are still being performed on a continuing basis by highway agencies (Holmes, 1962).

Toll Road Study

By the mid 1930s, there was considerable sentiment for a few long-distance, controlled-access highways connecting major cities. Advocates of such a highway system assumed that the public would be willing to finance much of its cost by tolls. The U.S Bureau of Public Roads was requested by President Roosevelt in 1937 to study the idea, and two years later it published the report, Toll Roads and Free Roads (U.S. Congress, 1939).

The study recommended the construction of a highway system to be comprised of direct, interregional highways with all necessary connections through and around cities. It concluded that this nationwide highway system could not be financed solely through tolls, even though certain sections could. It also recommended the creation of a Federal Land Authority empowered to acquire, hold, sell, and lease land. The report emphasized the problem of transportation within major cities and used the city of Baltimore as an example (Holmes, 1973).

Interregional Highway Report

In April 1941 President Roosevelt appointed the National Interregional Highway Committee to investigate the need for a limited system of national highways to improve the facilities available for interregional transportation. The staff work was done by the U.S. Public Roads Administration, which was the name of the Bureau of Public Roads at that time, and in 1944 the findings were published in the report, Interregional Highways (U.S. Congress, 1944). A system of highways, designated as the "National System of Interstate and Defense Highways," was recommended and authorized in the Federal Aid Highway Act of 1944. However, it was not until the Federal Aid Highway Act of 1956 that any significant work on the system began.

This study was unique in the annals of transportation planning and the implementation of its findings has had profound effects on American lifestyles and industry. The study brought planners, engineers, and economists together with the highway officials responsible for implementing highway programs. The final route choices were influenced as much by strategic necessity and such factors as population density, concentrations of manufacturing activity, and agricultural production as by existing and future traffic (Holmes, 1973).

The importance of the system within cities was recognized, but it was not intended that these highways serve urban commuter travel demands in the major cities. As stated in the report, "...it is important, both locally and nationally, to recognize the recommended system...as that system and those routes which best and most directly join region to region and major city to major city" (U.S. Congress, 1944).

The report recognized the need to coordinate with other modes of transportation and for cooperation at all levels of government. It reiterated the need for a Federal Land Authority with the power of excess condemnation and similar authorities at the state level.

3

BEGINNINGS OF URBAN
TRANSPORTATION PLANNING

Early Urban Travel Surveys

Most urban areas did not begin urban travel surveys until 1944. It was during that year that the Federal Aid Highway Act authorized the expenditure of funds on urban extensions of the federal-aid primary and secondary highway systems. Until that time there was a lack of information on urban travel that could be used for the planning of highway facilities. In fact, no comprehensive survey methods had been developed that could provide the required information. Because of the complex nature of urban street systems and the shifting of travel from route to route, traffic volumes were not a satisfactory guide to needed improvements. A study of the origins and destinations of trips and the basic factors affecting travel was needed (Holmes and Lynch, 1957).

The method developed to meet this need was the home-interview origin–destination survey. Household members were interviewed to obtain information on the number, purpose, mode, origin, and destination of all trips made on a particular day. These urban travel surveys were used in the planning of highway facilities, particularly expressway systems, and in determining design features. The U.S. Bureau of Public Roads published the first, *Manual of Procedures for Home Interview Traffic Studies*, in 1944 (U.S. Dept. of Commerce, 1944). In that year the interviewing technique was used in Tulsa, Little Rock, New Orleans, Kansas City, Memphis, Savannah, Oklahoma, and Lincoln.

Other elements of the urban transportation planning process were also being developed and applied in pioneering traffic planning studies. New concepts and techniques were being generated and refined in such areas as traffic counting, highway inventories and classification, highway capacity, pavement condition studies, cost estimating, and system planning. The first attempt to meld many of these elements into an urban transportation planning process was in the Cleveland Regional Area Traffic Study in 1927, which was sponsored by the U.S. Bureau of Public Roads. But, even in this study, traffic forecasting was a crude art using basically linear projections (Cron, 1975).

In the Boston Transportation Study, a rudimentary form of the gravity model was applied to forecast traffic in 1926 but the technique was not used in other areas. In fact, the 1930s saw little advancement in the techniques of urban transportation planning. It was during this period that the methodology of highway needs and financial studies was developed and expanded (U.S. Dept. of Transportation [DOT] 1979a).

By the 1940s it was apparent that if certain relationships between land use and travel could be measured, these relationships could be used as a means to project future travel. It remained for the development of the computer, with its ability to process large masses of data from these surveys, to permit estimation of these relationships between travel, land use, and other factors. The first major test using this approach to develop future highway plans was during the early 1950s in San Juan, Puerto Rico, and in Detroit (Silver and Stowers, 1964; Detroit Metropolitan Area Traffic Study, 1955/1956).

Early Transit Planning

During this period, transit planning was being carried out by operators as part of the regular activities of operating a transit system. Federal assistance was not available for planning or construction, and little federal interest existed in transit. In some urban areas, transit authorities were created to take over and operate the transit system. The Chicago Transit Authority was created in 1945, the Metropolitan Transit Authority in Boston in 1947, and the New York City Transit Authority in 1955.

It was at this time that the San Francisco Bay area began planning for a regional rapid transit system. In 1956, the Rapid Transit Commission proposed a 123 mile system in a five-county area. As a result of this study, the Bay Area Transit District (BARTD) was formed within the five counties. BARTD completed the planning for the transit system and conducted preliminary engineering and financial studies. In November 1962, the voters approved a bond issue to build a three-county, 75-mile system, totally with local funds (Homburger, 1967).

Dawn of Analytical Methods

Prior to the early 1950s, the results of early origin–destination studies were used primarily for describing existing travel patterns, usually in the form of trip origins and destinations and by "desire lines," indicating schematically the major spatial distribution of trips. Future urban travel volumes were developed by extending the past traffic growth rate into the future, merely an extrapolation technique. Some transportation studies used no projections of any sort and emphasized only the alleviation of existing traffic problems (U.S. DOT, 1967b).

Beginning in the early 1950s, new ideas and techniques were being rapidly generated for application in urban transportation planning. In 1950, the Highway Research Board published *Route Selection and Traffic Assignment* (Campbell, 1950), which was a compendium of correspondence summarizing practices in identifying traffic desire lines and linking origin–destination pairs. By the mid 1950s, Thomas Fratar at the Cleveland Transportation Study developed a computer method for distributing future origin–destination travel data using growth factors. In 1956 the Eno Foundation for Highway Traffic Control published *Highway Traffic Estimation* (Schmidt and Campbell, 1956), which documented the state of the art and highlighted the Fratar technique.

During this period the U.S. Bureau of Public Roads (BPR) sponsored a study on traffic generation at Columbia University, which was conducted by Robert Mitchell and Chester Rapkin. It was directed at improving the understanding of the relationship between travel and land use through empirical methods and included both persons and goods movement. Mitchell and Rapkin state as a major premise of their study:

> Despite the considerable amount of attention given in various countries to movement between place of residence and place of work, the subject has not been given the special emphasis suggested here; that is, to view trips between home and workplace as a "system of movement," changes in which may be related to land use change and to other changes in related systems of urban action or in the social structure. (Mitchell and Rapkin, 1954; p. 65)

They demonstrated an early understanding of many of the variables that effect travel patterns and behavior; for example:

> Systems of round trips from places of residence vary with the sex composition and age of the individual members of the household. The travel patterns of single individuals, young married couples, families with young children, and households consisting of aging persons all show marked differences in travel behavior. (Ibid., p. 70)

They also anticipated the contribution of social science methods to the understanding of travel behavior:

> However, inquiry into the motivations of travel and their correspondence with both behavior and the actual events which are consequences of travel would make great contributions to understanding why this behavior occurs, and thus to increase the possibility of predicting behavior. (Ibid., p. 54)

They concluded with a framework for analyzing travel patterns that included developing analytical relationships for land use and travel and then forecasting them as the basis for designing future transportation requirements.

Breakthroughs in Analytical Techniques

The first breakthrough in using an analytical technique for travel forecasting came in 1955 with the publication of a paper entitled, "A general theory of traffic movement," by Alan M. Voorhees (Voorhees, 1955). Voorhees advanced the gravity model as the means to link land use with urban traffic flows. Research had been proceeding for a number of years on a gravity theory for human interaction. Previously, the gravity analogy had been applied by sociologists and geographers to explain population movements. Voorhees used origin–destination survey data with driving time as the measure of spatial separation and estimated the exponents for a three-trip purpose gravity model. Others conducting similar studies soon corroborated these results (U.S. Dept. of Commerce, 1963a).

Another breakthrough soon followed in the area of traffic assignment. The primary difficulty in traffic assignment was evaluating the driver's choice of route between the origin and destination. Earl Campbell of the Highway Research Board proposed an "S" curve, which related the percent usage of a particular facility to a travel-time ratio. A number of empirical studies were undertaken to evaluate the theory using diversion of traffic to new expressways from arterial streets. From these studies, the American Association of State Highway Officials published a standard traffic diversion curve in, "A basis for estimating traffic diversion to new highways in urban areas," in 1952. However, traffic assignment was still largely a mechanical process requiring judgment (U.S. Dept. of Commerce, 1964).

Then in 1957 two papers were presented that discussed a minimum-impedance algorithm for road networks. One was titled, "The shortest path through a maze," by Edward F. Moore, and the second was, "The shortest route problem," by George B. Danzig. With such an algorithm, travel could then be assigned to minimum time paths using newly developed computers. The staff of the Chicago Area Transportation Study under Dr. J. Douglas Carroll, Jr. finally developed and refined computer programs that allowed the assignment of traffic for the entire Chicago region (U.S. Dept. of Commerce, 1964).

National Committee on Urban Transportation

While highway departments were placing major emphasis on arterial routes, city street congestion was steadily worsening. It was in this atmosphere that the Committee on Urban Transportation was created in 1954. Its purpose was, "to help cities do a better job of transportation planning through systematic collection of basic facts. . . to afford the public the best possible transportation at the least possible cost and aid in accomplishing desirable goals of urban renewal and sound urban growth'' (National Committee, 1958).

The committee was composed of experts in a wide range of fields, representing federal, state, and city governments, transit, and other interests. It developed a guidebook, *Better Transportation for Your City* (National Committee, 1958), designed to help local officials establish an orderly program of urban transportation planning. It was supplemented by a series of 17 procedure manuals describing techniques for planning highway, transit, and terminal improvements. The guidebook and manuals received national recognition. Even though the guidebook was primarily intended for the attention of local officials, it stressed the need for cooperative action, full communication between professionals and decision makers, and the development of transportation systems in keeping with the broad objectives of community development. It provided, for the first time, fully documented procedures for systematic transportation planning.

Housing Act of 1954

An important cornerstone of the federal policy concerning urban planning was Section 701 of the Housing Act of 1954. The act demonstrated congressional concern with urban problems and recognition of the urban planning process as an appropriate approach to dealing with such problems. Section 701 authorized the provision of federal planning assistance to state planning agencies, cities, and other municipalities having a population of less than 50,000 persons and, after further amendments, to metropolitan and regional planning agencies (Washington Center, 1970).

The intent of the act was to encourage an orderly process of urban planning to address the problems associated with urban growth and the formulation of local plans and policies. The act indicated that planning should occur on a region-wide basis within the framework of comprehensive planning.

Pioneering Urban Transportation Studies

The developments in analytical methodology began to be applied in pioneering urban transportation studies in the late 1940s and during the 1950s. Before these studies, urban transportation planning was based on existing travel demands or on travel forecasts using uniform growth factors applied on an area–wide basis.

The San Juan, Puerto Rico, transportation study, begun in 1948, was one of the earliest to use a trip generation approach to forecast trips. Trip generation rates were developed for a series of land-use categories stratified by general location, crude intensity measures, and type of activity. These rates were applied, with some modifications, to the projected land-use plan (Silver and Stowers, 1964).

The Detroit Metropolitan Area Traffic Study (DMATS) put together all the elements of an urban transportation study for the first time. It was conducted from 1953 to 1955 under Executive Director Dr. J. Douglas Carroll, Jr. The DMATS staff developed trip generation rates by land use category for each zone. Future trips were estimated from a land use forecast. The trip distribution model was a variant of the gravity model with airline distance as the factor to measure travel friction. Traffic assignment was carried out with speed and distance ratio curves. Much of the work was done by hand with the aid of tabulating machines for some of the calculations. Benefit/cost ratios were used to evaluate the major elements of the expressway network (DMATS, Parts I & II, 1955/1956; Silver and Stowers, 1964; Creighton, 1970).

In 1955 the Chicago Area Transportation Study (CATS) began under the direction of Dr. J. Douglas Carroll, Jr. It set the standard for future urban transportation studies. The lessons learned in Detroit were applied in Chicago with greater sophistication. CATS used the basic six-step procedure pioneered in Detroit: data collection, forecasts, goal formulation, preparation of network proposals, testing of proposals, and evaluation of proposals. Transportation networks were developed to serve travel generated by projected land-use patterns. They were tested using systems analysis considering the effect of each facility on other facilities in the network. Networks were evaluated based on economic efficiency—the maximum amount of travel carried at the least cost. CATS used trip generation, trip distribution, modal split, and traffic assignment models for travel forecasting. A simple land-use forecasting procedure was employed to forecast future land-use and activity patterns. The CATS staff made major advances in the use of the computer in travel forecasting (CATS, 1959-1962; Swerdloff and Stowers, 1966; Wells, et al., 1970).

Other transportation studies followed, including the Washington Area Traffic Study in 1955, the Baltimore Transportation Study in 1957, the Pittsburgh Area Transportation Study (PATS) in 1958, the Hartford Area Traffic Study in 1958, and the Penn–Jersey (Philadelphia) Transportation Study in 1959. All of these studies were transportation planning on a new scale. They were region-wide, multi-disciplinary undertakings involving large fulltime staffs. Urban transportation studies were carried out by ad hoc organizations with separate policy committees. They were not directly connected to any unit of government. Generally, these urban transportation studies were established for a limited time period with the objective of producing a plan and reporting on it. Such undertakings would have been impossible before the availability of computers (Creighton, 1970).

The resulting plans were heavily oriented to regional highway networks based primarily on the criteria of economic costs and benefits. Transit was given secondary consideration. New facilities were evaluated against traffic engineering improvements. Little consideration was given to regulatory or pricing approaches, or new technologies (Wells, et al., 1970).

These pioneering urban transportation studies set the content and tone for future studies. They provided the basis for the federal guidelines that were issued in the following decade.

Federal Aid Highway Act of 1956

During this early period in the development of urban transportation planning came the Federal Aid Highway Act of 1956. The act launched the largest public works program yet undertaken: construction of the National System of Interstate and Defense Highways. The act was the culmination of two decades of studies and negotiation. As a result of the Interregional Highways report, Congress had adopted a National System of Interstate Highways not to exceed 40,000 miles in the Federal Aid Highway Act of 1944. However, money was not authorized for construction of the system. Based on the recommendations of the U.S. Bureau of Public Roads and the Department of Defense, a 37,700-mile system was adopted in 1947. This network consisted primarily of the most heavily traveled routes of the Federal Aid Primary System. The remaining 2,300 miles were reserved for additional radials, bypass-loops, and circumferential routes in and adjacent to urban areas. Studies of urban area needs were made by the states with the cooperation and aid of city officials. The urban connections were formally designated in 1955 (U.S. Dept. of Commerce, 1957).

Funds were appropriated by then, but at very low levels: $25 million annually for 1952 and 1953 with a 50 percent federal share, and $175 million annually for 1954 and beyond with a 60 percent federal share. To secure a significant increase in funding, a major national lobbying effort was launched in 1952 by the Highway Users Conference under the title, "Project Adequate Roads." President Eisenhower appointed a national advisory committee under General Lucius D. Clay, which produced a report, *A Ten-Year National Highway Program*, in 1955. It recommended building a 37,000-mile Interstate System using bonds to fund the $23 billion cost (Kuehn, 1976).

Finally, with the Federal Aid Highway Act of 1956, construction of the National System of Interstate and Defense Highways shifted into high gear. The act increased the authorized system extent to 41,000 miles. This system was planned to link 90 percent of the cities with populations of 50,000 or greater and many smaller cities and towns. The act also authorized the expenditure of $24.8 billion in 13 fiscal years from 1957 to 1969 at a 90 percent federal share. The act provided construction standards and maximum sizes and weights of vehicles that could operate on the system. The system was to be completed by 1972 (Kuehn, 1976).

The companion Highway Revenue Act of 1956 increased federal taxes on gasoline and other motor fuels and excise taxes on tires and established new taxes on retreaded tires and a weight tax on heavy trucks and buses. It created the Highway Trust Fund to receive the tax revenue, which was dedicated solely for highway purposes. This provision broke with a long-standing congressional precedent not to earmark taxes for specific authorized purposes (U.S. Dept. of Commerce, 1957).

These acts have had a profound effect on urban areas. They established an assured funding source for highways, through user charges, at a time when federal funds were not available for mass transportation. They set a 90 percent federal share, which was far above the existing 50 percent share for other federal-aid highways. About 20 percent of the system mileage was designated as urban to provide alternative interstate service into, through, and around urban areas. These provisions dominated urban transportation planning for years to come and eventually caused the development of countervailing forces to balance the urban highway program.

Sagamore Conference on Highways and Urban Development

The availability of large amounts of funds from the 1956 Act brought immediate response to develop action programs. To encourage the cooperative development of highway plans and programs, a conference was held in 1958 in the Sagamore Center at Syracuse University (Sagamore, 1958).

The conference focused on the need to conduct the planning of urban transportation, including public transportation, on a region-wide, comprehensive basis in a manner that supported the orderly development of the urban areas. The conference report recognized that urban transportation plans should be evaluated through a grand accounting of benefits and costs that included both user and nonuser impacts.

The conference recommendations were endorsed and their implementation urged, but progress was slow. The larger urban areas were carrying out pioneering urban transportation studies, the most noteworthy being the CATS. But few of the smaller urban areas had begun planning studies due to the lack of capable staff to perform urban transportation planning.

To encourage smaller areas to begin planning efforts, the American Municipal Association, the American Association of State Highway Officials, and the National Association of County Officials jointly launched a program in early 1962 to describe and explain how to carry out urban transportation planning. This program was initially directed at urban areas under 250,000 in population (Holmes, 1973).

Housing Act of 1961

The first piece of federal legislation to deal explicitly with urban mass transportation was the Housing Act of 1961. This act was passed largely as a result of the growing financial difficulties with commuter rail services. The act inaugurated a small, low-interest loan program for acquisitions and capital improvements for mass transit systems and a demonstration program (Washington Center, 1970).

The act also contained a provision for making federal planning assistance available for "preparation of comprehensive urban transportation surveys, studies, and plans to aid in solving problems of traffic congestion, facilitating the circulation of people and goods in metropolitan and other urban areas and reducing transportation needs." The act permitted federal aid to "facilitate comprehensive planning for urban development, including coordinated transportation systems, on a continuing basis." These provisions of the act amended the Section 701 planning program that was created by the Housing Act of 1954.

4

URBAN TRANSPORTATION PLANNING COMES OF AGE

Urban transportation planning came of age with the passage of the Federal Aid Highway Act of 1962, which required that approval of any federal-aid highway project in an urbanized area of 50,000 or more in population be based on a continuing, comprehensive urban transportation planning process carried out cooperatively by states and local governments. This was the first legislative mandate requiring planning as a condition to receiving federal capital assistance funds. The U.S. Bureau of Public Roads (BPR) moved quickly to issue technical guidance interpreting the act's provisions.

Through the mid 1960s urban transportation planning went through what some have called its "golden age." Most urban areas were planning their regional highway system and urban transportation planning methodology had been designed to address this issue. The BPR carried out an extensive program of research, technical assistance and training to foster the adoption of this process and the new methodologies. These efforts completely transformed the manner in which urban transportation planning was performed. By the legislated deadline of July 1, 1965, all 224 then-existing urbanized areas that fell under the 1962 Act had an urban transportation planning process underway.

This was also a period in which there was early recognition of the need for a federal role in urban mass transportation. This role, however, was to remain limited for a number of years to come.

Joint Report on Urban Mass Transportation

In March 1962 a joint report on urban mass transportation was submitted to President Kennedy, at his request, by the Secretary of Commerce and the Housing and Home Finance Administrator (U.S. Congress, Senate, 1962). This report integrated the objectives for highways and mass transit, which were comparatively independent up to that point but growing closer through cooperative activities. The report was in large part based on a study completed in 1961 by the Institute for Public Administration (IPA) entitled *Urban Transportation and Public Policy*. The IPA report strongly recommended that urban transportation was a federal concern and supported the need for transportation planning.

The general thrust of the report to Congress, as it related to planning, can be summarized by the following excerpt from the transmittal letter:

> Transportation is one of the key factors in shaping our cities. As our communities increasingly undertake deliberate measures to guide their development and renewal, we must be sure that transportation planning and construction are integral parts of general development planning and programming. One of our main recommendations is that federal aid for urban transportation should be made available only when urban communities have prepared or are actively preparing up-to-date general plans for the entire urban area which relate transportation plans to land-use and development plans.
>
> The major objectives of urban transportation policy are the achievement of sound land-use patterns, the assurance of transportation facilities for all segments of the population, the improvement of overall traffic flow, and the meeting of total transportation needs at minimum cost. Only a balanced transportation system can attain these goals—and in many urban areas this means an extensive mass transportation network fully integrated with the highway and street system. But mass transportation in recent years experienced capital consumption rather than expansion. A cycle of fare increases and service cuts to offset loss of ridership followed by further declines in use points clearly to the need for a substantial contribution of public funds to support needed mass transportation improvements. We therefore recommend a new program of grants and loans for urban mass transportation. (U.S. Congress, Senate, 1962)

President Kennedy's Transportation Message

In April 1962 President Kennedy delivered his first message to Congress on the subject of transportation. Many of the ideas related to urban transportation in the message drew upon the previously mentioned joint report. The President's message recognized the close relationship between the community development and the need to properly balance the use of private automobiles and mass transportation to help shape and serve urban areas. It also recognized the need to promote economic efficiency and livability of urban areas. It also recommended continued close cooperation between the Department of Commerce and the Housing and Home Finance Administration (HHFA) (Washington Center, 1970).

This transportation message opened a new era in urban transportation and lead to passage of two landmark pieces of legislation: the Federal Aid Highway Act of 1962 and the Urban Mass Transportation Act of 1964.

Federal Aid Highway Act of 1962

The Federal Aid Highway Act of 1962 was the first piece of federal legislation to mandate urban transportation planning as a condition for receiving federal funds in urbanized areas. It asserted that federal concern in urban transportation was to be integrated with land development and provided a major stimulus to urban transportation planning. Section 9 of the act, which is now Section 134 of Title 23 states:

It is declared to be in the national interest to encourage and promote the development of transportation systems embracing various modes of transport in a manner that will serve the states and local communities efficiently and effectively. (U.S. DOT, 1980a)

This statement of policy directly followed from the recommendations of the Sagamore conference and President Kennedy's Transportation Message. Moreover, the section directed the Secretary of Commerce to cooperate with the states:

. . .in the development of long-range highway plans and programs which are properly coordinated with plans for improvements in other affected forms of transportation and which are formulated with due consideration to their probable effect on the future development of the urban area. . . (U.S. DOT, 1980a)

The last sentence of the section, which required that urban highway construction projects be based upon a planning process, legislated the planning requirement:

After July 1, 1965, the Secretary shall not approve under section 105 of this title any programs for projects in any urban area of more than fifty thousand population unless he finds that such projects are based on a continuing, comprehensive transportation planning process carried out cooperatively by states and local communities in conformance with the objectives stated in this section. (U.S. DOT, 1980a)

Two features of the act are particularly significant with respect to the organizational arrangements for carrying out the planning process. First, it called for a planning process in urban areas rather than cities, which set the scale at the metropolitan or regional level. Second, it called for the process to be carried on cooperatively by the states and local communities. Because qualified planning agencies to mount such a transportation planning process were lacking in many urban areas, the BPR required the creation of planning agencies or organizational arrangements that would be capable of carrying out the required planning process. These planning organizations quickly came into being because of the growing momentum of the highway program and the cooperative financing of the planning process by the HHFA and the BPR (Marple, 1969).

In addition, the act restricted the use of the 1.5 percent planning and research funds to only those purposes. If not used for planning and research, the state would lose the funds. Previously, a state could request that these funds be used instead for construction. This provision created a permanent, assured funding source for planning and research activities. In addition, the act provided that a state could spend another 0.5 percent at their option for planning and research activities.

Hershey Conference on Urban Freeways

In response to the growing concern about freeway construction in urban areas, the Hershey Conference on Freeways in the Urban Setting was convened in June 1962 (Hershey Conference, 1962). It concluded, "Freeways cannot be planned independently of the areas through which they pass. The planning concept should extend to the entire sector of the city within the environs of the freeway." The conference recommendations reinforced the need to integrate highway planning and urban development.

The findings recognized that this planning should be done as a team effort that draws upon the skills of engineers, architects, city planners, and other specialists. Freeway planning must integrate the freeway with its surroundings. When properly planned, freeways provide an opportunity to shape and structure the urban community in a manner that meets the needs of the people who live, work, and travel in these areas. Further, the planning effort should be carried out in a manner that involves participation by the community (Hershey Conference, 1962).

Implementation of the 1962 Federal Aid Highway Act

The BPR moved quickly to implement the planning requirements of the 1962 Federal Aid Highway Act. Instructional Memorandum 50-2-63, published in March 1963 (U.S. Dept of Commerce, 1963c) and later superseded by Policy and Procedure Memorandum 50-9 (U.S. DOT, 1967a), interpreted the act's provisions related to a "continuing, comprehensive, and cooperative" (3C) planning process. "Cooperative" was defined to include not only cooperation between the federal, state, and local levels of government but also among the various agencies within the same level of government. "Continuing" referred to the need to periodically reevaluate and update a transportation plan. "Comprehensive" was defined to include the basic ten elements of a 3C planning process for which inventories and analyses were required:

1. Economic factors affecting development
2. Population
3. Land use
4. Transportation facilities including those for mass transportation
5. Travel patterns
6. Terminal and transfer facilities
7. Traffic control features
8. Zoning ordinances, subdivision regulations, building codes, etc.
9. Financial resources
10. Social and community-value factors, such as preservation of open space, parks and recreational facilities; preservation of historical sites and buildings; environmental amenities; and aesthetics.

These memoranda and further refinements and expansions upon them covered all aspects for organizing and carrying out the 3C planning process.

Through its Urban Planning Division, under Garland E. Marple, the BPR carried out a broad program to develop planning procedures and computer programs, write procedural manuals and guides, teach training courses, and provide technical assistance. The effort was aimed at developing urbanized area planning organizations, standardizing, computerizing, and applying procedures largely created in the late 1950s, and disseminating knowledge of such procedures.

The BPR defined the various steps in a 3C planning process. These steps had been pioneered by the urban transportation planning studies that were carried out during the 1950s. It was an empirical approach that required a substantial amount of data and several years to complete. The process consisted of: establishing an organization to carry out the planning process; development of local goals and objectives; surveys and inventories of existing conditions and facilities; analyses of current conditions and calibration of forecasting techniques; forecasting of future activity and travel; evaluation of alternative transportation networks resulting in a recommended transportation plan; staging of the transportation plan; and identification of resources to implement it. The product of these 3C planning studies was generally an elaborate report(s) describing the procedures, analyses, alternatives and recommended plans.

To foster the adoption of these technical procedures, the BPR released a stream of procedural manuals that became the technical standards for many years to come: *Calibrating and Testing a Gravity Model for Any Size Urban Area* (July 1963); *Calibrating and Testing a Gravity Model with a Small Computer* (October 1963); *Traffic Assignment Manual* (June 1964); *Population Forecasting Methods* (June 1964); *Population, Economic, and Land Use Studies in Urban Transportation Planning* (July 1964); *The Standard Land Use Coding Manual* (January 1965); *The Role of Economic Studies in Urban Transportation Planning* (August 1965); *Traffic Assignment and Distribution for Small Urban Areas* (September

1965); *Modal Split—Documentation of Nine Methods for Estimating Transit Usage* (December 1966); and *Guidelines for Trip Generation Analysis* (June 1967).

The BPR developed a two-week "Urban Transportation Planning Course" that was directed at practicing planners and engineers. It covered organizational issues and technical procedures for carrying out a 3C planning process as it had been conceptualized by the BPR. The course used the BPR manuals as textbooks and supplemented them with lecture notes to keep the information current and to cover material not in manual form. In addition, personnel from the BPR provided hands-on technical assistance to state and local agencies in applying these new procedures to their own areas.

This effort to define the "3C planning process," to develop techniques for performing the technical activities, and to provide technical assistance completely transformed the manner in which urban transportation planning was performed. By the legislated deadline of July 1, 1965, all the 224 existing urbanized areas which fell under the 1962 Act had an urban transportation planning process underway (Holmes, 1973).

Conventional Urban Travel Forecasting Process

The 3C planning process included four technical phases: collection of data, analysis of data, forecasts of activity and travel, and evaluation of alternatives. Central to this approach was the urban travel forecasting process (Fig. 4.1). The process used mathematical models that allowed the simulation and forecasting of current and future travel. This permitted the testing and evaluation of alternative transportation networks.

The four-step urban travel forecasting process consisted of trip generation, trip distribution, modal split, and traffic assignment. These models were first calibrated to replicate existing travel using actual survey data. These models were then used to forecast future travel. The forecasting process began with an estimate of the variables that determine travel patterns including the location and intensity of land use, social and economic characteristics of the population, and the type and extent of transportation facilities in the area. Next, these variables were used to estimate the number of trip origins and destinations in each subarea of a region (i.e., the traffic analysis zone), using a trip-generation procedure. A trip-distribution model was used to connect the trip ends into an origin-destination trip pattern. This matrix of total vehicle trips was divided into highway and transit trips using a modal-split model. The matrices of highway and transit trips were assigned to routes on the highway and transit networks, respectively, by means of a traffic assignment model (U.S. DOT, 1977).

In using these models to analyze future transportation networks, forecasts of input variables were used for the year for which the networks were being tested. Travel forecasts were then prepared for each transportation alternative to determine traffic volumes and levels of service. Usually only the modal-split

FIGURE 4.1.   Urban travel forecasting process

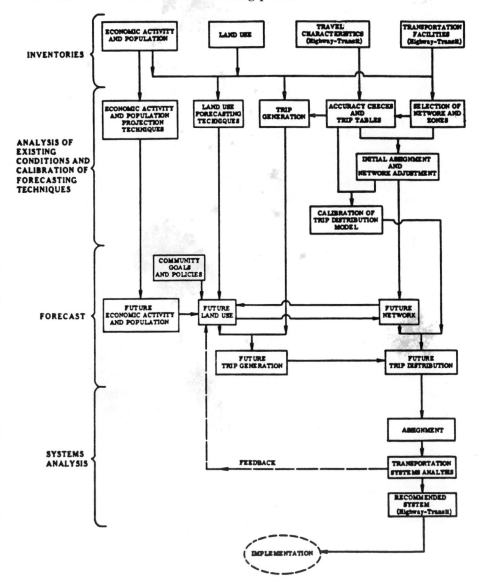

and traffic-assignment models were rerun for additional networks after a future-year forecast had been made for the first network. But occasionally the trip-distribution model was also rerun.

Travel forecasting on a region-wide scale required a large computing capability. The first generation of computers had become available in the mid 1950s. The BPR had taken advantage of them and adapted a telephone-routing algorithm for traffic assignments purposes that would operate on the IBM 704 computer. Additional programs were generated to perform other functions. The second generation of computers, circa 1962, provided increased capabilities. The library of computer programs was rewritten for the IBM 709 computer and then for the IBM 7090/94 system. The BPR worked with the Bureau of Standards in developing, modifying, and testing these programs. Some programs were also developed for the IBM 1401 and 1620 computers. This effort was carried out over a number of years, and by 1967 the computer package contained about 60 programs (U.S. DOT, 1977).

This approach to travel forecasting, which later became known as the "conventional urban travel forecasting process," came quickly into widespread use. The procedures had been specifically tailored to the tasks of region-wide urban transportation planning and BPR provided substantial assistance and oversight in applying them. Moreover, there were no other procedures generally available and urban transportation study groups that chose not to use them had to develop their own procedures and computer programs.

Urban Mass Transportation Act of 1964

The first real effort to provide federal assistance for urban mass transportation development was the passage of the Urban Mass Transportation Act of 1964. The objective of the act, still in the spirit of President Kennedy's Transportation Message, was "...to encourage the planning and establishment of area-wide urban mass transportation systems needed for economical and desirable urban development" (U.S. DOT, 1979b).

The act authorized federal capital grants for up to two-thirds of the net project cost of construction, reconstruction, or acquisition of mass transportation facilities and equipment. Net project cost was defined as that portion of the total project cost that could not be financed readily from transit revenues. However, the federal share was to be held to 50 percent in those areas that had not completed their comprehensive planning process, that is, had not produced a plan. All federal funds had to be channeled through public agencies. Transit projects were to be initiated locally.

A program of research, development, and demonstrations was also authorized by the 1964 act. The objective of this program was to "...assist in the reduction of transportation needs, the improvement of mass transportation service, or the contribution of such service toward meeting total urban transportation needs at minimum cost" (U.S. DOT, 1979b).

Congress, however, did not authorize much money to carry out this legislation. Not more than $150 million per year was authorized under the 1964 act and the actual appropriations fell short of even that amount (Smerk, 1968).

Williamsburg Conference on Highways and Urban Development

By 1965 there was concern that planning processes were not adequately evaluating social and community values. Few planning studies had developed goal-based evaluation methodologies. A second conference on Highways and Urban Development was held in Williamsburg, Virginia, to discuss this problem (Highways and Urban Development, 1965). The conference concluded that transportation must be directed toward raising urban standards and enhancing aggregate community values. Transportation values such as safety, economy, and comfort are part of the total set of community values and should be weighted appropriately.

The conference resolutions highlighted the need to identify urban goals and objectives that should be used to evaluate urban transportation plans. It emphasized that many values may not be quantifiable but, nonetheless, should not be ignored. The conference also endorsed the concept of making maximum use of existing transportation facilities through traffic management and land use controls.

5

IMPROVED INTERGOVERNMENTAL COORDINATION

As federal programs expanded in the provision of urban development and transportation facilities, intergovernmental coordination became more difficult and time consuming. Several measures were taken to develop mechanisms to alleviate this problem. One result was to encourage broader, multifunctional planning agencies.

Housing and Urban Development Act of 1965

The Housing and Urban Development Act of 1965 created the Department of Housing and Urban Development (HUD) to better coordinate urban programs at the federal level. In addition, the act amended the Section 701 urban planning assistance program established under the Housing Act of 1954 by authorizing grants to be made to "...organizations composed of public officials whom he (the Secretary of HUD) finds to be representative of the political jurisdictions within a metropolitan area or urban region...." for the purposes of comprehensive planning (Washington Center, 1970).

This provision encouraged the formation of regional planning organizations controlled by elected rather than appointed officials. It gave impetus to the formation of such organizations as councils of governments (COGs). It also encouraged local governments to cooperate in addressing their problems in a regional context.

Department of Transportation Act of 1966

In 1966 the Department of Transportation (DOT) was created to coordinate transportation programs and to facilitate development and improvement of coordinated transportation service utilizing private enterprise to the maximum extent feasible. The Department of Transportation Act declared that the nation required fast, safe, efficient, and convenient transportation at the lowest cost consistent with other national objectives including the conservation of natural resources. DOT was directed to provide leadership in the identification of transportation problems and solutions, stimulate new technological advances, encourage cooperation among all interested parties, and recommend policies and programs to accomplish these objectives.

Section 4(f) of the act required the preservation of natural areas. It prohibited the use of land for a transportation project from a park, recreation area, wildlife and waterfowl refuge, or historic site unless there was no feasible and prudent alternative and the project was planned in such a manner as to minimize harm to the area. This was the earliest statutory language directed at minimizing the negative effects of transportation construction projects on the natural environment.

The DOT Act left unclear, however, the division of responsibility for urban mass transportation between DOT and HUD. It took more than a year for DOT and HUD to come to an agreement on their respective responsibilities. This agreement, known as Reorganization Plan No. 2, took effect in July 1968. Under it, DOT assumed responsibility for mass transportation capital grants, technical studies, and managerial training grant programs subject to HUD certification of the planning requirements for capital grant applications. Research and development (R&D) was divided up. DOT assumed R&D responsibility for improving the operation of conventional transit systems and HUD assumed R&D responsibility for urban transportation as it related to comprehensive planning. Joint responsibility was assigned for R&D on advanced technology systems. The Reorganization Plan also created the Urban Mass Transportation Administration (UMTA) (Miller, 1972).

1966 Amendments to the Urban Mass Transportation Act of 1964

To fill several gaps in the 1964 Urban Mass Transportation Act, a number of amendments were passed in 1966. One created the technical studies program, which provided federal assistance up to a two-thirds federal matching share for planning, engineering, and designing of urban mass transportation projects or other similar technical activities leading to application for a capital grant.

Another section authorized grants to be made for management training. A third authorized a project to study and prepare a program of research for developing new systems of urban transportation. This section resulted in a report to Congress in 1968, *Tomorrow's Transportation: New Systems for the Urban Future* (Cole, 1968), which recommended a long-range balanced program for research on hardware, planning, and operational improvements. It was this study that first brought to public attention many new systems such as dial-a-bus, personal rapid transit, dual mode, pallet systems, and tracked air-cushioned vehicle systems.

This study was the basis for numerous research efforts to develop and refine new urban transportation technologies that would improve on existing ones.

Demonstration Cities and Metropolitan Development Act of 1966

Section 204 of the Demonstration Cities and Metropolitan Development Act of 1966 was significant in asserting federal interest in improving the coordination of public facility construction projects to obtain maximum effectiveness of federal spending and to relate such projects to area-wide development plans. It required that all applications for the planning and construction of facilities be submitted to an area-wide planning agency for review and comment. The object of this section of the act was to encourage the coordination of planning and construction of physical facilities in urban areas. Procedures to implement this act were issued by the Bureau of the Budget in Circular No. 82. In response to these review requirements, many urban areas established new planning agencies or reorganized existing agencies to include elected officials on their policy boards (Washington Center, 1970).

Dartmouth Conference on Urban Development Models

Land use planning models were developed as an adjunct to transportation planning to provide forecasts of population, employment, and land use for transportation forecasting models. From the mid 1950s there was rapid development in the field stimulated by newly available computers and advances in operations research and systems analysis (Putman, 1979). Developments were discussed at a seminar at the University of Pennsylvania in October 1964 that was documented in a special issue of the *Journal of the American Institute of Planners* (Harris, 1965).

By 1967 the Land Use Evaluation Committee of the Highway Research Board determined that there was need for another assessment of work in the field, which was progressing in an uncoordinated fashion. A conference was held in Dartmouth, New Hampshire, in June 1967 to identify the areas of research that were most needed (Hemmens, 1968).

The conferees recommended that agencies sponsoring research on land use models, generally the federal government, expand the capabilities of their in-house staff to handle these models. They recommended steps to improve data acquisition and handling. Further research on broader models that included social goals was recommended. Conferees recommended that research on the behavioral aspects of the individual decision units be conducted. Concern was expressed about bridging the gap between modelers and decision makers. Professional standards for design, calibration, and use of models were also encouraged (Hemmens, 1968).

The early optimism in the field faded as the land development models did not perform up to the expectations of researchers and decision makers, particularly at the small area level. Modelers had underestimated the task of simulating complex urban phenomena. Many of these modeling efforts were performed by planning agencies that had to meet unreasonable time deadlines (Putman, 1979). Models had become more complex with larger data requirements as submodels were added to encompass more aspects of the urban development process. They were too costly to construct and operate, and many still did not produce usable results. By the late 1960s land-use modeling activity in the United States entered a period of dormancy that continued until the mid 1970s.

Reserved Bus Lanes

As construction of the Interstate highway progressed, highway engineers came under increasing criticism for providing underpriced facilities that competed unfairly with transit service. Critics were also concerned that the 3C planning process was not giving sufficient attention to transit options in the development of long-range urban transportation plans.

The first official response to this criticism came in April 1964 in a speech by E. H. Holmes, Director of Planning for the Bureau of Public Roads. Mr. Holmes stated: "Since over three-quarters of transit patrons ride on rubber tires, not on steel rails, transit has to be for highways, not against them. And vice versa, highways have to be for transit, not against it, for the more that travelers patronize transit the easier will be the highway engineer's job." He went on to advocate the use of freeways by buses in express service. This would increase bus operating speeds, reduce their travel times, and thereby make bus service more competitive with car travel. The BPR position was that the reservation of a lane for buses was reasonable if its usage by bus passengers exceeded the number of persons that would be moved in the same period in cars, for example, 3,000 per hour (Holmes, 1964).

This position was formalized in *Instructional Memorandum* (IM) 21-13-67, "Reserved Bus Lanes," issued by the Federal Highway Administration (FHWA) in August 1967. In addition to reiterating the warrant for reserving lanes for buses, the IM stated the warrant for preferential use of lanes by buses. Under preferential use, other vehicles would be allowed to use the lane but only in such numbers that they do not degrade the travel speeds of the buses. The number of other vehicles would be controlled by metering their flow onto the lane. The total number of persons using the preferential lanes was to be greater than would be accommodated by opening the lanes to general traffic.

The FHWA actively promoted the use of exclusive and preferential bus treatments. Expenditures for bus priority projects on arterial highways, including loading platforms and shelters, became eligible for federal aid highway funds under the Traffic Operations Program to Improve Capacity and Safety (TOPICS), which was initiated as an experimental program in 1967. Reserved lanes for buses on freeways were eligible under the regular federal aid highway programs.

Many urban areas adopted bus priority techniques to increase the carrying capacity of highway facilities and make transit service more attractive at a limited cost. By 1973 one study reported on more than 200 bus priority projects in the United States and elsewhere. These included busways on exclusive rights-of-way and on freeways, reserved freeway lanes and ramps, bus malls, reserved lanes on arterial streets, traffic signal preemption, and supporting park-and-ride lots and central city terminals (Levinson, 1973).

National Highway Needs Studies

The expected completion of the Interstate highway system in the mid-1970s lead to consideration of new directions for the federal-aid highway program. Recognizing the need for information on which to formulate future highway programs, the U.S. Senate, in section 3 of the Senate Joint Resolution 81 (approved August 28, 1965) called for a biennial reporting of highway needs beginning in 1968.

In April 1965, the Bureau of Public Roads had requested the states to prepare estimates of future highway needs for the period 1965–1985. The states were given only a few months to prepare the estimates and they relied upon available data and rapid estimating techniques. The results were documented in the *1968 National Highway Needs Report*. The estimated cost of $294 billion to meet the anticipated highway needs was a staggering sum. It included another 40,000 of freeways in addition to the 41,000 miles in the Interstate system (U.S. Congress, 1968a). The supplement to the report recommended the undertaking of a nationwide functional highway classification study as the basis for realigning the federal-aid highway systems (U.S. Congress, 1968b).

The 1968 report focused greater attention on urban areas than in the past. The supplement recommended that a larger share of federal-aid highway funds should be made available to urban areas. As a means to accomplish this, the supplement discussed expanding the urban extensions of the primary and secondary highway systems to include all principal arterial routes into a federal-aid urban system. To overcome the difficulties of urban area decision making among fragmented local governments, it suggested requiring the establishment of area-wide agencies to develop five-year capital improvement programs. The agencies would be governed by locally elected officials (U.S. Congress, 1968b).

The supplement also recommended the use of federal-aid highway funds for parking research and development projects, and for construction of fringe parking facilities. The establishment of a revolving fund for advance acquisition of right-of-way was recommended as well. The supplement advocated joint development adjacent to or using airspace above or below highways. Such projects should be coordinated jointly by DOT and HUD (U.S. Congress, 1968b).

Many of the recommendations in the *Supplement to the 1968 National Highway Needs Report* were incorporated into the Federal-Aid Highway Acts of 1968 and 1970. Section 17 of the 1968 act called for a systematic nationwide functional highway classification study in cooperation with state highway departments and local governments. The manual for this functional classification study stated that, "All existing public roads and streets within a State are to be classified on the basis of the most logical usage of existing facilities to serve present travel and land use" (U.S. Dept. of Transportation, 1969b). This was the first major study to collect detailed functional system information on a nationwide basis.

The supplement to the *1970 National Highway Needs Report* detailed the results of the 1968 functional classification study which covered existing facilities under current conditions of travel and land use. The results showed that there was wide variation among states in the coincidence of highways classified functionally and which federal-aid system they were on. This disparity was greater in urban areas than in rural areas. The report demonstrated that arterial highways carried the bulk of highway travel. For example, in urban areas in 1968, arterial highways constituted 19 percent of the miles of facilities and carried 75 percent of the vehicle miles of travel [Figure 5.1] (U.S. Congress, 1970).

The 1972 National Highway Needs Report covered the results of the 1970-1990 functional classification study. It combined a projected functional classification for 1990 with a detailed inventory and needs estimate for all functional classes including local roads and streets. It recommended the realignment of federal-aid highway systems based upon functional usage in a subsequent year such as 1980. This recommendation for realignment was incorporated into the Federal-Aid Highway Act of 1973. Highway needs were estimated for the twenty-year period to 1990 under nationally uniform "minimum tolerable conditions." Of the estimated $592 billion in needs, 43 percent were on federal-aid systems as they existed in 1970. Over 50 percent of these needs were considered to be "backlog," that is, requiring immediate attention (U.S. Congress, 1972a and 1972b).

The 1974 National Highway Needs Report updated the needs estimates that were reported in the 1972 report. The 1974 Highway Needs Study was conducted as part of the 1974 National Transportation Study. The 1974 highway report analyzed the sensitivity of the needs estimates to the changes of reduced forecasted travel and a lower level of service than minimum tolerable conditions. The report clarified that the highway needs estimates were dependent upon the specific set of standards of highway service and highway design on which they are based.

The highway needs studies represented an ongoing process to assess the nation's highway system and quantify the nature and scope of future highway requirements. The studies were carried out as cooperative efforts of the federal,

FIGURE 5.1. **National distribution of miles versus vehicle-miles of travel served on the highway systems in urban areas: 1968**

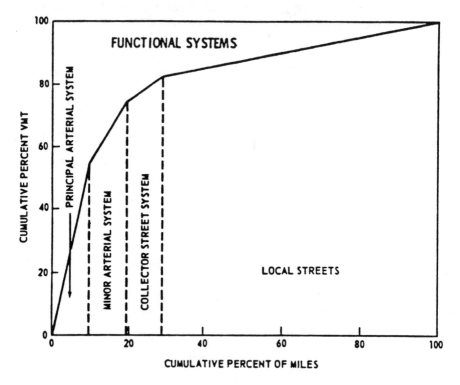

state and local governments. The extensive involvement of state and local governments lent considerable credibility to the studies. Consequently, the highway needs reports had a major influence on highway legislation, and the structure and funding of highway programs (U.S. Congress, 1975).

Federal Aid Highway Act of 1968

The Federal Aid Highway Act of 1968 established the Traffic Operations Program to Improve Capacity and Safety (TOPICS). It authorized $200 million each for fiscal years 1970 and 1971. The federal matching share was set at 50 percent. The program was designed to reduce traffic congestion and facilitate the flow of traffic in urban areas. Prior to the act, the Bureau of Public Roads had initiated TOPICS as an experimental program. IM 21-7-67, which established guidelines for TOPICS, divided urban streets into two categories. Those on the federal aid Primary and Secondary systems were considered Type 1. Other major streets were under Type 2. Only traffic operations improvements were allowed on Type 2 systems (Gakenheimer and Meyer, 1977).

The TOPICS program grew out of a long history of the BPR's efforts to expand the use of traffic engineering techniques. In 1959 the BPR sponsored the Wisconsin Avenue Study to demonstrate the effectiveness of various traffic management methods when applied in a coordinated fashion (U.S. Dept. of Commerce, 1962).

TOPICS projects were to result from the 3C urban transportation planning process. By October 1969 there were 160 cities actively involved in TOPICS and another 96 cities in preliminary negotiations expected to result in active projects. Even so, the level of planning detail for TOPICS projects was not totally compatible with the regional scale of the planning process (Gakenheimer and Meyer, 1977).

The TOPICS program was reauthorized for fiscal years 1972 and 1973 at $100 million per year. But the Federal Aid Highway Act of 1973 ended further authorizations and merged the TOPICS systems into the new federal aid urban system. TOPICS had accomplished its objective of increasing the acceptance of traffic engineering techniques as a means of improving the efficiency of the urban transportation system. It also played an important role in encouraging the concept of traffic management (Gakenheimer and Meyer, 1977).

In addition to launching the TOPICS program, the Federal Aid Highway Act of 1968 incorporated several provisions designed to protect the environment and reduce the negative effects of highway construction. The Act repeated the requirement in Section 4(f) of the Department of Transportation Act of 1966 on the preservation of public park and recreation lands, wildlife and waterfowl refuges, and historic sites to clarify that the provision applied to highways. Moreover the Act required public hearings on the economic, social, and environmental effects of proposed highway projects and their consistency with local urban goals and objectives. The Act also established the highway beautification program. In addition a highway relocation assistance program was authorized to provide payments to households and businesses displaced by construction projects. Additionally, a revolving fund for the advanced acquisition of right-of-way was established to minimize future dislocations due to highway construction and reduce the cost of land and clearing it. Also, the Act authorized funds for a fringe parking demonstration program.

Many of the provisions of the Act were early responses to the concern for environmental quality and for ameliorating the negative effects of highway construction.

Intergovernmental Cooperation Act of 1968

Section 204 of the Demonstration Cities and Metropolitan Act was the forerunner of much more extensive legislation, adopted in 1968, designed to coor-

dinate federal grant-in-aid programs at federal and state levels. The Intergovernmental Cooperation Act of 1968 required that federal agencies notify the
governors or legislatures of the purpose and amounts of any grants-in-aid to their
states. The purpose of this requirement was to make it possible for states to plan
more effectively for their overall development (Washington Center, 1970).

"Continuing" Urban Transportation Planning

By 1968 most urbanized areas had completed or were well along in their
3C planning process. The Federal Highway Administration turned its attention
to the "continuing" aspect of the planning process. In May 1968 IM 50-4-68,
"Operations Plans for 'Continuing' Urban Transportation Planning" was issued.
The IM required the preparation of an operations plan for continuing transportation planning in these areas. The objective was to maintain the responsiveness
of planning to the needs of local areas and to potential changes (U.S. DOT,
1968).

The operations plans were to address the various items needed to perform
continuing planning, including: the organizational structure; scope of activities
and the agencies that were responsible; a description of the surveillance methodology to identify changes in land development and travel demand; a description of land use and travel forecasting procedures; and work remaining on the
ten basic elements of the 3C planning process (U.S. DOT, 1968).

Guidelines were provided identifying the five elements considered essential
for a continuing planning process (Fig. 5.2). The "surveillance" element focused
on monitoring changes in the area in development, sociodemographic characteristics, and travel. "Reappraisal" dealt with three levels of review of the transportation forecasts and plan to determine if they were still valid. Every five years
the plan and forecast were to be updated to retain a 20-year time horizon. The
third element, "service," was to assist agencies in the implementation of the
plan. The "procedural development" element emphasized the need to upgrade
analysis techniques. Last was the publication of an "annual report" on these activities as a means of communicating with local officials and citizens (U.S. DOT,
1968).

Extensive training and technical assistance was provided by the FHWA to
shift urban transportation planning into a continuing mode of operation.

Bureau of the Budget's Circular No. A-95

To implement the 1968 Intergovernmental Cooperation Act, the Bureau of
the Budget issued Circular No. A-95 in July 1969, which superseded Circular
No. A-82. This circular required that the governor of each state designate a
"clearinghouse" at the state level and for each metropolitan area. The function

FIGURE 5.2. The continuing urban transportation planning process

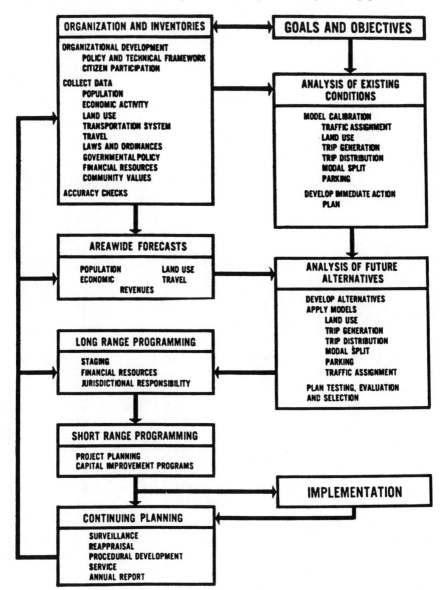

FIGURE 5.3. Comparison of 204 review process and project notification and review system

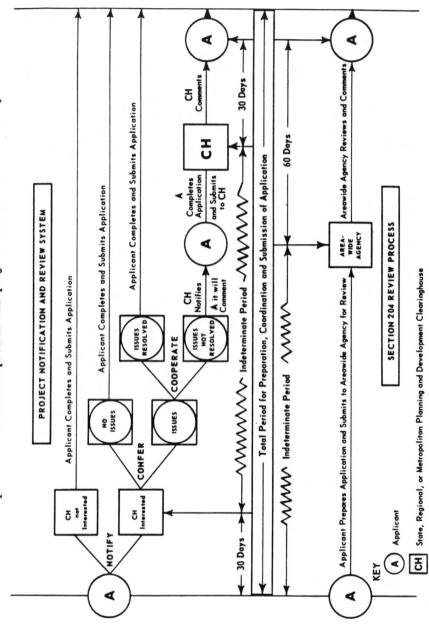

of these clearinghouses was to review and comment on projects proposed for federal aid in terms of their compatibility with comprehensive plans and to coordinate among agencies having plans and programs that might be affected by the projects. These clearinghouses had to be empowered under state or local laws to perform comprehensive planning in an area (Washington Center, 1970).

The circular established a project notification and review system (PNRS), which specified how the review and coordination process would be carried out and the amount of time for each step in the process (Fig. 5.3). The PNRS contained an "early warning" feature that required that a local applicant for a federal grant or loan notify the state and local clearinghouses at the time it decided to seek assistance. The clearinghouse had 30 days to indicate further interest in the project or to arrange to provide project coordination. This regulation was designed to alleviate the problem many review agencies had of learning of an application only after it had been prepared, and thereby having little opportunity to help shape it (Washington Center, 1970).

Circular No. A-95 provided the most definitive federal statement of the process through which planning for urban areas should be accomplished. Its emphasis was not on substance but on process and on the intergovernmental linkages required to carry out the process.

The various acts and regulations to improve intergovernmental program coordination accelerated the creation of broader multifunctional agencies. At the state level, 39 Departments of Transportation had been created by 1977. Most of the departments had multimodal planning, programming, and coordinating functions. At the local level, there was a growing trend for transportation planning to be performed by comprehensive planning agencies, generally those designated as the A-95 clearinghouse (Advisory Commission, 1974).

6

THE ENVIRONMENT AND CITIZEN INVOLVEMENT

During the decade of the 1960s, the growing concern for environmental quality put considerable pressure on the planning process and its ability to adapt to change. Public attention became focused on the issues of air and water pollution; dislocation of homes and businesses; preservation of parkland, wildlife refuges, and historic sites; and the overall ecological balance in communities and their capacity to absorb disruption. Moreover, citizens were concerned that changes were being made to their communities without their views being considered. The federal role in these matters, which had begun modestly in previous years, broadened and deepened during this period.

Citizen Participation and the Two-Hearing Process for Highways

Citizen reaction to highway projects usually was most vocal at public hearings. It became clear that citizens could not effectively contribute to a highway decision by the time the project had already been designed. Many of the concerns related to the basic issue of whether to build the highway project at all and the consideration of alternative modes of transportation. Consequently, in early 1969, the Federal Highway Administration (FHWA) revised Policy and Procedure Memorandum (PPM) 20-8, "Public Hearings and Location Approval." It established a two-hearing process for highway projects, replacing the previous single hearing, which occurred late in the project development process.

The first "corridor public hearing" was to be held before the route location decision was made and was designed to afford citizens the opportunity to comment on the need for and location of the highway project. The second "highway design public hearing" was to focus on the specific location and design features. This PPM also required the consideration of social, economic, and environmental effects prior to submission of a project for federal aid. (U.S. DOT, 1976b).

It was recognized that even a two-hearing process did not provide adequate opportunity for citizen involvement and, worse, provided a difficult atmosphere for dialogue. In late 1969 the basic guidelines for the 3C planning process were amended to require citizen participation in all phases of the planning process from the setting of goals through the analysis of alternatives. Consequently, it became the responsibility of the planning agency to seek out public views.

National Environmental Policy Act of 1969

The federal government's concern for environmental issues dated back to the passage of the Air Quality Control Act of 1955, which directed the Surgeon General to conduct research to abate air pollution. Through a series of acts since that time, the federal government's involvement in environmental matters had broadened and deepened.

In 1969 a singularly important piece of environmental legislation was passed, the National Environmental Policy Act of 1969 (NEPA). This act presented a significant departure from prior legislation in that it enunciated for the first time a broad national policy to prevent or eliminate damage to the environment. The act stated that it was national policy to "encourage productive and enjoyable harmony between man and his environment."

Federal agencies were required under the act to use a systematic interdisciplinary approach to the planning and decision making that affected the environment. It also required that an environmental impact statement (EIS) be prepared for all legislation and major federal actions that would affect the environment significantly. The EIS was to contain information on the environmental impacts of the proposed action, unavoidable impacts, alternatives to the action, the relationship between short-term and long-term impacts, and irretrievable commitments of resources. The federal agency was to seek comments on the action and its impacts from affected jurisdictions and make all information public.

The act also created the Council on Environmental Quality to implement the policy and advise the President on environmental matters.

Environmental Quality Improvement Act of 1970

The Environmental Quality Improvement Act of 1970 was passed as a companion to the NEPA. It established the Office of Environmental Quality under the Council of Environmental Quality. The office was charged with assisting federal agencies in evaluating present and proposed programs, and with promoting research on the environment.

These two acts dealing with the environment mark the first reversal in over a decade of the trend to decentralize decision making to the state and local levels of government. It required the federal government to make the final determination on the trade-off between facility improvements and environmental quality. Further, it created a complicated and expensive process by requiring the preparation of an EIS and the seeking of comments from all concerned agencies. In this manner the acts actually created a new planning process in parallel with the existing urban transportation planning process.

Clean Air Act Amendments of 1970

The Clean Air Act Amendments of 1970 reinforced the central position of the federal government to make final decisions affecting the environment. This act created the Environmental Protection Agency (EPA) and empowered it to set ambient air quality standards. Required reductions in new automobile emissions were also specified in the act. The act authorized the EPA to require states to formulate implementation plans describing how they would achieve and maintain the ambient air quality standards. In 1971 the EPA promulgated national ambient air quality standards and proposed regulations on state implementation plans (SIPs) to meet these standards (U.S. DOT, 1975b).

The preparation, submission, and review of the SIPs occurred outside the traditional urban transportation planning process and, in many instances, did not involve the planning agencies developing transportation plans. This problem became particularly difficult for urban areas that could not meet the air quality standards even with new automobiles that met the air pollution emission standards. In these instances, transportation control plans (TCPs) were required that contained changes in urban transportation systems and their operation to effect the reduction in emissions. Rarely were these TCPs developed jointly with those agencies developing urban transportation plans. It took several years of dialogue between these air pollution and transportation planning agencies to mediate joint plans and policies for urban transportation and air quality.

Another impact of the environmental legislation, particularly the Clean Air Act, was the increased emphasis on short-term changes in transportation systems. In that the deadline for meeting the ambient air quality standards was fairly short, EPA was primarily concerned with actions that could affect air quality in that time frame. The actions precluded major construction and generally focused on low capital and traffic management measures. Up to that time, urban transportation planning had been focused on long-range (20 years or more) planning (U.S. DOT, 1975b).

Boston Transportation Planning Review

The results of many urban transportation planning studies called for major expansions of given areas' freeway systems along with other highway improvements. Public transportation was often projected to have a minimal role in the area's future. In these urban transportation plans, many of the highway improvements were to be located in built up areas where they would cause major disruptions and dislocations. As public awareness to social and environmental concerns grew in many urban areas, so too did the opposition to transportation plans that contained recommendations for major expansions of the highway system. When faced with these circumstances, urban areas were forced to reevaluate their plans. The prototype for these reevaluations was the Boston Transportation Planning Review (BTPR).

The long-range plan for the Boston region published in 1969 contained recommendations for a comprehensive network of radial and circumferential highways and substantial improvements to the existing mass transportation system. Much of the freeway portion of the plan was included as part of the Interstate highway system. Many of the recommended highways were contained in the earlier 1948 plan, which was typical of urban transportation plans of this period. Opposition to the 1969 plan developed even before it was published, especially from the affected communities (Humphrey, 1974).

Governor Francis Sargent ordered a moratorium on major highway construction in February 1970, shortly after the Boston City Council had already done so. He announced a major reevaluation of transportation policy for the Boston area and created the BTPR as an independent entity reporting directly to the governor to address the area's transportation issues.

The BTPR lasted about 18 months, during which time numerous transportation alternatives were identified and evaluated by an interdisciplinary team of professionals. The work was accomplished in an atmosphere of open and participatory interaction among planners, citizens, and elected officials. The BTPR lead to the decision made by the governor not to build additional freeways within the Boston core. Instead, the major emphasis was on a mix of arterials, special purpose highways, and major improvements in the mass transportation system (Humphrey, 1974).

There were several hallmarks of this new form of the urban transportation planning process, termed by Alan Altshuler, who chaired the BTPR, the "open study." First and foremost was the extensive involvement of professionals, citizens, interest groups, and decision makers in all aspects of the restudy. Second, transit options were evaluated on an equal footing with highway options. Third, the restudy focused on both the broader region-wide scale and the finer community level scale. Fourth, there was less reliance on computer models for analysis and a more open attitude toward explaining the analytical methodology to the nontechnical participants. Fifth, the study used a wider range of evaluation criteria that accounted for more social and environmental factors. Sixth, decision makers were willing to step in and make decisions at points where the process had reached a stalemate (Gakenheimer, 1976; Allen, 1985).

The BTPR occurred at the height of the citizen participation movement in a highly charged atmosphere outside the mainstream of decision making in Boston. Although it is unlikely that such a study will be repeated elsewhere in the same manner, the BTPR has left a permanent impact on urban transportation. The legacy of the BTPR has been to demonstrate a more open form of planning and decision making that has greater concern for social and environmental impacts and the opinions of those affected by transportation improvements.

Conference on Urban Commodity Flow

The urban transportation planning processes and methodologies that had been developed through the decade of the 1960s emphasized passenger movement. Little attention was given to the problems of commodity movements in urban areas. The majority of studies of urban goods movement had been limited to those related to trucks. Data on commodity movements was seldom collected because of the difficulty in tracking the movements and the lack of available methods (Chappell and Smith, 1971).

In recognition of the need for more information and better planning concerning the movement of goods in urban areas, a Conference on Urban Commodity Flow was convened at Airlie House in Warrentown, Virginia on December 6–9, 1970. Initially, the conference was to focus on information and techniques to forecast urban commodity movement. But, as planning for the conference progressed, there emerged a need for a more fundamental understanding of commodity movements and the economic, social, political and technological forces that affected them (Highway Research Board, 1971a).

The conference revealed the lack of information on highway goods movement and the need for such information to make informed policy decisions on investment and regulation. The various viewpoints on the problems of urban commodity flow were explored. Planners, shippers, government agencies, freight carriers, and citizens saw the problems and consequences differently. With so many actors, the institutional issues were considered to be too complex to mount effective strategies to address the problems (Highway Research Board, 1971a).

The conferees concluded that goods movement needed more emphasis in the urban transportation planning process and that techniques for forecasting goods movement needed to be developed. The regulations and programs of federal, state, and local agencies needed to be coordinated to avoid conflicting effects on the goods movement industry that were not in the best interest of the public. Greater efforts were called for to explore means of reducing the economic, social, and environmental costs of goods movement in urban areas (Highway Research Board, 1971a).

This conference directed attention to the neglect of goods movement in the urban transportation planning process, and the complexity of the goods movement issue. It generated more interest and research in the subject and focused on the opportunity to develop strategies to deal with urban goods movement problems.

7

BEGINNINGS OF MULTIMODAL URBAN TRANSPORTATION PLANNING

By the late 1960s, the urban transportation planning process was receiving criticism on a number of issues. It was criticized for inadequate treatment of social and environmental impacts. The planning process had still not become multimodal and was not adequately evaluating a wide range of alternatives. Planning was focused almost exclusively on long-range time horizons, and the technical procedures to carry out planning were too cumbersome, time-consuming, and rigid to adapt to new issues quickly.

During the 1970s actions were taken to address these criticisms. Legislation was passed that increased the capital funds available for mass transportation and provided federal assistance for operating costs. Greater flexibility was permitted in the use of some highway funds, including their use on transit projects. These provisions placed transit on a more equal footing with highways and considerably strengthened multimodal planning and implementation.

Urban Mass Transportation Assistance Act of 1970

The Urban Mass Transportation Assistance Act of 1970 was another landmark in federal financing for mass transportation. It provided the first long-term commitment of federal funds. Until the passage of this act, federal funds for mass transportation had been limited. It was difficult to plan and implement a program of mass transportation projects over several years because of the uncertainty of future funding.

The 1970 act implied a federal commitment for the expenditure of at least $10 billion over a 12-year period to permit confident and continuing local planning and greater flexibility in program administration. The act authorized $3.1 billion to finance urban mass transportation beginning in fiscal year 1971. It permitted the use of "contract authority" whereby the Secretary of Transportation was authorized to incur obligations on behalf of the United States with Congress pledged to appropriate the funds required to liquidate the obligations. This provision allowed long-term commitments of funds to be made.

This act also established a strong federal policy on transportation for elderly and handicapped persons:

> ...elderly and handicapped persons have the same right as other persons to utilize mass transportation facilities and services; that special efforts shall be made in the planning and design of mass transportation facilities and services so that the availability to elderly and handicapped persons to mass transportation which they can effectively utilize will be assured....(U.S. DOT, 1979b)

The act authorized that 2 percent of the capital grant and 1.5 percent of the research funds might be set aside and used to finance programs to aid elderly and handicapped persons.

The act also added requirements for public hearings on the economic, social and environmental impacts of a proposed project and on its consistency with the comprehensive plan for the area. It also required an analysis of the environmental impacts of the proposed project and for the Secretary of Transportation to determine that there was no feasible or prudent alternative to any adverse impact that might result.

Federal Aid Highway Act of 1970

The Federal Aid Highway Act of 1970 established the federal aid urban highway system. The system in each urban area was to be designed to serve major centers of activity and to serve local goals and objectives. Routes on the system were to be selected by local officials and state departments cooperatively. This provision significantly increased the influence of local jurisdictions in urban highway decisions. The influence of local officials in urban areas was further strengthened by an amendment to Section 134 on urban transportation planning:

> No highway project may be constructed in any urban area of 50,000 population or more unless the responsible local officials of such urban area...have been consulted and their views considered with respect to the corridor, the location and the design of the project (U.S. DOT, 1980a)

Funds for the federal aid urban system were to be allocated to the states on the basis of total urban population within the state. The act also authorized the expenditure of highway funds on exclusive or preferential bus lanes and related facilities. This could only be done if the bus project reduced the need for additional highway construction or if no other highway project could provide the person-carrying capacity of the bus project. There had to be assurances, as well, that the transit operator would utilize the facility. An additional provision of the act authorized expenditures of highway funds on fringe and corridor parking facilities adjacent to the federal aid urban system that were designed in conjunction with public transportation services.

This act also incorporated a number of requirements related to the environment. One required the issuance of guidelines for full consideration of economic, social and environmental impacts of highway projects. A second related to the promulgation of guidelines for assuring that highway projects were consistent with SIPs developed under the Clean Air Act.

As a result of the 1970 highway and transit acts, projects for both modes would have to meet similar criteria related to impact assessment and public hearings. The highway act also increased the federal matching share to 70 percent for all non-Interstate highways, making it comparable to the 66.67 percent federal share for mass transportation capital projects. In addition, the highway act legally required consistency between SIPs and urban highway plans.

Mt. Pocono Conference on Urban Transportation Planning

In recognition of the widespread awareness that urban transportation planning had not kept pace with changing conditions, a conference on Organization for Continuing Urban Transportation Planning was held at Mt. Pocono, Pennsylvania, in 1971. The focus of this conference was on multimodal transportation planning evolving from the earlier conferences that had focused on highway planning and the separation between planning and implementation (Highway Research Board, 1973a).

The conference recommended close coordination of planning efforts as a means of achieving orderly development of urban areas and relating the planning process more closely to decision-making processes at all levels of government. It urged that urban planning be strengthened through state enabling legislation and bolstered by equitable local representation. Further, citizen participation should occur continually throughout the planning process but should not be considered as a substitute for decision making by elected officials (Advisory Commission, 1974).

All comprehensive and functional planning, including multimodal transportation planning, should be integrated, including the environmental impact assessment process. The planning process should continually refine the long-range regional transportation plan at the sub-area scale and focus on a 5- to 15-year time frame so that planning would be more relevant to programming and project implementation. Transportation planning should consider service levels consistent with local goals, and a wide range of alternatives should be evaluated. The impact of changes in the transportation system should be monitored to improve future decision making and planning efforts (Advisory Commission, 1974).

The conference report went on to urge that this more inclusive kind of planning be supported by flexible funding from the federal government. This was to be done to avoid a preference for any mode so as not to unbalance specific urban transportation decisions contrary to local goals and priorities. The conference also supported additional resources for planning, research, and training.

DOT Initiatives Toward Planning Unification

The U.S. Department of Transportation had been working for several years on integrating the individual modal planning programs. In 1971 the DOT established a trial program of intermodal planning in the field. The overall objective of the program was to integrate the modal planning programs at the urban-area level rather than at the federal level. With the successful completion of the trial program, the DOT implemented the program on a permanent basis by establishing intermodal planning groups (IPGs) in each of the 10 DOT regions. The IPGs were charged wtih responsibility for obtaining and reviewing an annual unified work program for all transportation planning activities in an urban area; for obtaining agreement on a single recipient agency for areawide transportation planning grants in each urban area; and, for obtaining a short-term (3–5-year) transportation capital improvement program, updated annually, from each recipient agency (U.S. DOT and HUD, 1974).

Also in 1971 a DOT transportation planning committee was established to promote a coordinated department-wide process for urban-area and statewide transportation planning and for unified funding of such planning. As a result of the efforts of the committee, a DOT order was issued in 1973 that required that all urbanized areas submit annual unified work programs for all transportation planning activities as a condition for receiving any DOT planning funds. These work programs had to include all transportation-related planning activities, identification of the agency responsible for each activity, and the proposed funding sources. The work programs were used to rationalize planning activities and joint funding under the DOT planning assistance programs (U.S. DOT and HUD, 1974).

Process Guidelines for Highway Projects

The Federal Aid Highway Act of 1970 required that guidelines be issued to assure that possible adverse economic, social and environmental effects were considered in developing highway projects and that decisions on these projects were made in the best overall public interest. Initially guidelines were developed specifying requirements and procedures for evaluating the effects in each of the impact areas. These guidelines were presented and discussed at a Highway Research Board Workshop during July 1971 in Washington, D.C. The primary conclusion of the workshop was that full consideration of adverse impacts and of decisions in the best overall public interest could not be assured by extensive technical standards. It would depend upon the attitudes, capabilities, organization, and procedures of the highway agencies responsible for developing the projects (U.S. Congress, 1972).

Based on the workshop recommendations and other comments, the emphasis of the guidelines was shifted to the process used in developing highway projects. In September 1972 FHWA issued PPM 90-4, "Process Guidelines (Economic, Social, and Environmental Effects of Highway Projects)." These guidelines required each state to prepare an Action Plan spelling out the organizational arrangement, the assignment of responsibilities, and the procedures to be followed in developing projects in conformance with the law. The Action Plan had to address the process for identification of social, economic, and environmental impacts, considerations of alternative courses of action, use of a systematic interdisciplinary approach, and the involvement of other agencies and the public. Flexibility was provided to the States to develop procedures that were adjusted to their own needs and conditions.

The use of process guidelines was a further evolution of the manner in which highway projects were developed. The staffs of highway agencies were exposed to the views of other agencies and the public. Professionals with skills in the social and environmental areas were brought into the process. Gradually the project development process became more open and embraced a broader range of criteria in reaching decisions.

Williamsburg Conference on Urban Travel Forecasting

By the latter part of the 1960s use of the conventional urban travel forecasting procedures pioneered in the late 1950s and early 1960s was widespread but criticism of them was growing. Critics argued that coventional procedures were time-consuming and expensive to operate and required too much data. The procedures had been designed for long-range planning of major facilities and were not suitable for evaluation of the wider range of options that were of interest, such as low-capital options, demand-responsive systems, pricing alternatives, and vehicle restraint schemes. Policy issues and options had changed, but travel demand forecasting techniques had not.

These issues were addressed at a conference on Urban Travel Demand Forecasting held at Williamsburg, Virginia, in December 1972, sponsored by the Highway Research Board and the U.S. Department of Transportation. The conference concluded that there was a need for travel forecasting procedures that were sensitive to the wide range of policy issues and alternatives to be considered, quicker and less costly than conventional methods, more informative and useful to decision makers, and in a form that nontechnical people could understand. Further, that improvements in methodology were urgently needed, and that significant improvements in capabilities could be achieved within three years based on the results of available research (Brand and Manheim, 1973).

The conference recommended several simultaneous paths to improve travel forecasting capabilities. First was to upgrade existing methodology with the results of recent research. Second was to pilot-test emerging procedures in several urban areas. Third was research to improve the understanding of travel behavior, including before/after studies, consumer theory, psychological theory, and location behavior. Fourth, research was needed to transform the results of travel behavior research into practical forecasting techniques. Fifth, a two-way dissemination program was necessary to get new methods into the field and for the results of these applications to flow back to the researchers to improve the methods (Brand and Manheim, 1973).

The conferees were optimistic that the conversion to new, improved behavioral methods was soon to be at hand. They did recognize that a substantial amount of research was going to be necessary. And in fact the Williamsburg conference did launch a decade of extensive research and activity to disaggregate urban travel demand forecasting.

Federal Aid Highway Act of 1973

The Federal Aid Highway Act of 1973 contained two provisions that increased the flexibility in the use of highway funds for urban mass transportation in the spirit of the Mt. Pocono conference. First, federal aid urban system funds could be used for capital expenditures on urban mass transportation projects. This provision took effect gradually, but was unrestricted starting in Fiscal Year 1976. Second, funds for Interstate highway projects could be relinquished and replaced by an equivalent amount from the general fund and spent on mass transportation projects in a particular state. The relinquished funds reverted back to the Highway Trust Fund.

This opening up of the Highway Fund for urban mass transportation was a significant breakthrough sought for many years by transit supporters. These changes provided completely new avenues of federal assistance for funding urban mass transportation.

The 1973 act had other provisions related to urban mass transportation. First, it raised the federal matching share for urban mass transportation capital projects from 66.67 to 80 percent, except for urban system substitutions, which remain at 70 percent. Second, it raised the level of funds under the UMTA capital grant program by $3 billion, to $6.1 billion. Third, it permitted expenditure of highway funds for bus-related public transportation facilities, including fringe parking on all federal-aid highway systems.

The act called for realigning all federal-aid systems based on functional usage. It authorized expenditures on the new federal aid urban system and modified several provisions related to it. "Urban" was defined as any area of 5,000 or more in population. Apportioned funds for the system were earmarked for urban areas of 200,000 or more population. Most important, it changed the relationship between the state and local officials in designating routes for the system. It authorized local officials in urbanized areas to choose routes with the concurrence of state highway departments (Parker, 1977).

Two additional provisions related directly to planning. For the first time urban transportation planning was funded separately: 0.5 percent of all federal-aid funds were designated for this purpose and apportioned to the states on the basis of urbanized-area population. These funds were to be made available to the metropolitan planning organizations (MPOs) responsible for comprehensive transportation planning in urban areas.

The 1973 Federal Aid Highway Act took a significant step toward integrating and balancing the highway and mass transportation programs. It also increased the role of local officials in the selection of urban highway projects and broadened the scope of transportation planning by MPOs.

1972 and 1974 National Transportation Studies

Although urban transportation planning had been legislatively required for over a decade, the results had not been used in the development of national transportation policy. Beyond that, a composite national picture of these urban transportation plans did not exist, even though they were the basis for capital expenditure decisions by the federal government. In the early 1970s, the Department of Transportation conducted two national transportation studies to inventory and assess the current and planned transportation system as viewed by the states and urban areas.

The two studies differed in their emphasis. The 1972 National Transportation Study obtained information on the existing transportation system as of 1970, the transportation needs for the 1970–1990 period, and short-range (1974–1978) and long-range (1979–1990) capital improvement programs under three federal funding assumptions (U.S. DOT, 1972b). The study showed that the total transportation needs of the states and urban areas exceeded the financial resources of the nation to implement them and discussed the use of low-capital alternatives to improve the productivity of the existing transportation system, particularly in urban areas.

The 1974 National Transportation Study related more closely to the ongoing urban transportation planning processes (U.S. DOT, 1975b). It obtained information on the 1972 inventories, long-range plans (1972–1990), and short-range programs (1972–1980) for the transportation system in a more comprehensive manner than did the 1972 study. The transportation system for all three periods was described in terms of the supply of facilities, equipment, and services, travel demand, system performance, social and environmental impacts, and capital and operating costs. Information on low-capital alternatives and new technological systems was also included. The 1972–1980 program was based on a forecast of federal funds that could reasonably be expected to be available and an estimate of state and local funds for the period (Weiner, 1974). This study again demonstrated that the long-range plans were overly ambitious in terms of the financial resources that might be available for transportation. Further, it showed that even after the expenditure of vast amounts of money for urban transportation, urban transportation systems would differ little in character in the foreseeable future (Weiner, 1975b).

The National Transportation Study process introduced the concept of tying state and urban transportation planning into national transportation planning and policy formulation. It stressed multimodal analysis, assessment of a wide range of measures of the transportation system, realistic budget limitations on plans and programs, and increasing the productivity of the existing transportation system. Although these concepts were not new, the National Transportation studies marked the first time that they had been incorporated into such a vast national planning effort (Weiner, 1976).

National Mass Transportation Assistance Act of 1974

The National Mass Transportation Assistance Act of 1974 authorized for the first time the use of federal funds for transit operating assistance. It thereby continued the trend to broaden the use of federal urban transportation funds and provide state and local officials more flexibility. This act was the culmination of a major lobbying effort by the transit industry and urban interests to secure federal operating assistance for transit.

The act authorized $11.8 billion over a 6-year period. Almost $4 billion was to be allocated to urban areas by a formula based on population and population density. The funds could be used for either capital projects or operating assistance. The funds for areas over 200,000 in population were attributable to those areas. The funds were to be distributed to "designated recipients" jointly agreed to by the governor, local elected officials, and operators of publicly-owned mass transportation services. For areas under 200,000 in population, the governor was designated to allocate the funds. Of the remaining $7.8 billion, $7.3 billion was made available for capital assistance at the discretion of the Secretary of Transportation and the remainder was for rural mass transportation. Funds used for capital projects were to have an 80 percent federal matching share. Operating assistance was to be matched 50 percent by the federal government.

Section 105(g) of the act required applicants for transit projects to meet the same planning statute as Section 134 of the highway act. Finally, highway and transit projects were subject to the same long-range planning requirement. Although many urbanized areas already had a joint highway/transit planning process, this section formalized the requirement for multimodal transportation planning.

The act also required transit systems to charge elderly and handicapped persons fares that were half regular fares when they traveled in off-peak hours. This was a further condition to receiving federal funds.

The act created a new Section 15 that required the Department of Transportation to establish a data-reporting system for financial and operating information and a uniform system of accounts and records. After July 1978 no grant could be made to any applicant unless they were reporting data under both systems.

PLANPAC and UTPS Batteries of Computer Programs

The computer programs developed and maintained by BPR during the 1960s were essential to most urban transportation planning studies, which generally did not have the time and resources to develop their own programs. The battery had been written for the most part by the U.S. Bureau of Standards and consisted of 60 single purpose computer programs. Toward the end of the decade of the 1960s, new batteries of computer programs were being developed for transportation planning for the recently introduced third generation of computers, the IBM 360 (U.S. DOT, 1977).

The highway planning package, known as PLANPAC, was rewritten to take advantage of the new capabilities of these computers. Most highway agencies were acquiring IBM 360s for their own computer installations and would soon be able to use the new computers. PLANPAC included computer programs to analyze survey data, develop and apply trip generation relationships, calibrate and apply trip distribution models, perform traffic assignment, evaluate networks, and for plotting utility programs to handle data sets (U.S. DOT, 1977).

New programs continued to be written and added to PLANPAC. In 1974 the FHWA completed a reorientation of the package. Many of the programs in PLANPAC that were not associated with the traditional four-step urban travel forecasting process were shifted to BACKPAC. These included computer programs for traffic signal optimization, parking studies, highway capacity analysis, carpool matching, micro traffic analysis, land-use forecasting, and freeway management. This resulted in 59 programs being retained in PLANPAC and 244 programs being included in BACKPAC.

A battery of computer programs for transit system planning was also developed during the mid 1960s by the U.S. Department of Housing and Urban Development, which administered the federal transit program at that time. The battery was first written for the IBM 7090/94 computers and consisted of 11 multi-purpose programs. About 1973 UMTA assumed responsibility for the HUD transit planning package and released an enhanced version for the IBM 360 as the UMTA Transportation Planning System (UTPS). The programs were designed for network analysis, travel demand estimation, sketch planning, and data manipulation. The programs were compatible and communicated through a common data base.

In 1976 the FHWA decided not to perform any further developments for PLANPAC but instead join with UMTA to support the UTPS package whose name was changed to Urban Transportation Planning System. FHWA did make a commitment to maintain and support PLANPAC as long as users needed it. The first release of the UMTA/FHWA multimodal UTPS was in 1976. A 1979/80 release provided additional capabilities and contained 20 programs.

The development and support of computer programs by FHWA and UMTA substantially assisted urban transportation planning studies in performing their various analytical and planning functions. These computer batteries facilitated the use of conventional planning techniques and furthered this style of urban transportation planning.

8

TRANSITION TO
SHORT-TERM PLANNING

As planning for the Interstate Highway System was being completed, attention turned to increasing the productivity and efficiency of existing facilities. In planning for major new regional transportation facilities, many urban areas had neglected maintaining and upgrading other facilities. However, environmental concerns, the difficulty of building innercity freeways, renewed interest in urban mass transit, and the energy crisis gave added impetus to the focus on more immediate problems. Signs were becoming evident of the changing emphasis to shorter-term time horizons and the corridor level in transportation planning. Gradually, planning shifted to maximizing the use of the existing system with a minimum of new construction. Further, the connection was strengthened between long-term planning and the programming of projects (Weiner, 1982).

Arab Oil Embargo

In October 1973 the Organization of Petroleum Exporting Countries (OPEC) embargoed oil shipments to the United States and in doing so, began a new era in transportation planning. The importance of oil was so paramount to the economy and, in particular, the transportation sector that oil shortages and price increases gradually became one of the major issues in transportation planning.

The immediate reaction to the oil embargo was to address the specific emergency. President Nixon signed the Emergency Petroleum Allocation Act of 1973 in November of that year, which established an official government allocation plan for gasoline and home heating fuel. It regulated the distribution of refined petroleum products by freezing the supplier-purchaser relationships and specifying a set of priority users. The act also established price controls on petroleum. It gave the President authority to set petroleum prices, not to exceed $7.66 a barrel. This authority was to terminate on September 30, 1981.

The Emergency Highway Energy Conservation Act, signed on January 2, 1974, established a national 55 miles per hour speed limit to reduce gasoline consumption. It was extended indefinitely on January 4, 1975 (U.S. DOT, 1979c). It also provided that federal aid highway funds could be used for ridesharing demonstration programs.

As the immediate crisis abated, the focus shifted to longer-term actions and policies to reduce the nation's dependence on oil, especially imported oil. The Energy Policy and Conservation Act of 1975 was passed by Congress to ensure that automobile gasoline consumption would be reduced to the lowest level possible and to promote energy conservation plans. As directed, the U.S. Department of Transportation through the National Highway Traffic Safety Administration (NHTSA) promulgated regulations that required the corporate average fuel economy (CAFE) for all automobile manufacturers (domestic and imported) be raised from 18.0 miles per gallon in 1978 to 27.5 in 1985 and beyond (U.S. DOT, 1979c).

Reaction to the energy crisis of 1973/74 evolved slowly at the local level as information and analysis tools gradually appeared. Most local planning agencies knew little about energy consumption and conservation and needed to learn about this new issue that had been thrust upon them. It was not until the second crisis in 1979 with fuel shortages and sharply increasing prices that energy issues were thoroughly integrated into urban transportation planning.

Joint Highway/Transit Planning Regulations

The UMTA and FHWA had worked for several years on joint regulations to guide urban transportation planning. Final regulations were issued to take effect in October 1975 (U.S. DOT, 1975a). They superseded all previous guidelines, policies, and regulations issued on urban transportation planning by the UMTA and FHWA. The regulations provided for the joint designation of MPOs to carry out planning and required agreements on the division of responsibility where the MPOs and A-95 agencies were different. A multiyear prospectus and annual unified work program had to be submitted specifying all transportation-related planning activities for an urban area as a condition for receiving federal planning funds. (See Fig. 8.1).

The urban transportation planning process was required to produce a long-range transportation plan, which had to be reviewed annually to confirm its validity. The transportation plan had to contain a long-range element and a shorter-range "transportation systems management element" (TSME) for improving the operation of existing transportation systems without new facilities.

A multiyear "transportation improvement program" (TIP) also had to be developed consistent with the transportation plan. The TIP had to include all highway and transit projects to be implemented within the coming five years. It thereby became the linkage between the planning and programming of urban transportation projects. It also brought together all highway and transit projects

FIGURE 8.1. Joint FHWA/UMTA urban transportation planning process

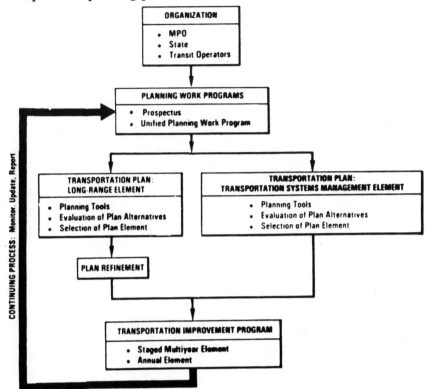

into a single document that could be reviewed and approved by decision makers. The TIP had to contain an "annual element" that would be the basis for the federal funding decisions on projects for the coming year.

The regulations provided for a joint annual certification of the planning process. This certification was required as a condition for receiving federal funds for projects. The regulations incorporated previously legislated requirements related to social, economic, and environmental impact analysis, air quality planning, and the elderly and handicapped.

These joint regulations applied to all urban highway and transit programs including those for transit operating assistance. They represented the most important action up to that time to bring about multimodal urban transportation planning and programming of projects. They changed the emphasis from long-term planning to shorter-range transportation system management, and provided a stronger linkage between planning and programming. These regulations were another turning point in the evolution of urban transportation planning that set the tone for the next several years.

Model 13(c) Labor Protection Agreement for Operating Assistance

Section 13(c) was included in the Urban Mass Transportation Act of 1964 to protect employees in the transit industry from potential adverse effects of federal transit assistance. At the time, federal assistance was in the form of capital grants and loans that could be used for public acquisition of private operations. A major concern was the loss of collective bargaining rights when employees entered the public sector.

Section 13(c) required an applicant for federal assistance to make arrangements to protect the interests of employees. Employee protection arrangements under Section 13(c) included: (1) preservation of rights under existing contracts; (2) continuation of collective bargaining rights; (3) protection of employees against a worsening of their positions; (4) assurances of employment or reemployment for existing employees; and (5) paid training or retraining programs.

The Secretary of Labor was responsible for determining whether these arrangements were fair and equitable. There had been an evolution in the administration of Section 13(c) since it was enacted. Originally the Department of Labor (DOL) only required a statement that the interests of employees would not be adversely affected by the Federal grant. By 1966, however, there had evolved detailed 13(c) agreements that were the result of collective bargaining between grant applicants and the employee representatives. These 13(c) agreements were subject to renegotiation with each new grant.

With the passage of the National Mass Transportation Assistance Act of 1974, federal funds became available for operating assistance under the Section 5 Formula Grant program. Grants for operating assistance were also required to comply with the Section 13(c) provisions. To facilitate processing of these operating assistance applications, organized labor, the American Public Transit Association (APTA) and the DOL developed a national model 13 (c) agreement pertaining to such agreements. The model agreement was signed in July 1975 by APTA, the Amalgamated Transit Union, and the Transport Workers Union of America. APTA established a procedure under which individual transit properties could affiliate themselves with the agreement and, thereby, become eligible for coverage by it for operating assistance applications (Lieb, 1976).

The model section 13(c) agreement for transit operating assistance reduced the time and effort of individual transit properties and labor representatives to negotiate agreement and accelerated the use of federal funds for operating assistance.

Office of Technology Assessment's Report on Automated Guideway Transit

By the time the report *Tomorrow's Transportation: New Systems for the Urban Future* (Cole, 1968) was published in 1968, UMTA barely had a research program in the area of new urban transit technologies. A small grant had been made for development of Westinghouse's Transit Expressway and several new system feasibility studies were begun in 1967. By 1970 decisions had been reached to proceed with funding of three major automated guideway transit (AGT) demonstration projects—the Transpo 72 exhibition and two other demonstrations (U.S. Congress, OTA, 1975).

Transpo 72 was held at the Dulles International Airport near Washington, D.C. in the spring of 1972. Four companies built and operated prototype AGT systems for public demonstration. In 1971 UMTA awarded a grant to the Vought Corporation to build a group rapid transit (GRT) system, Airtrans, as the internal circulation system for the Dallas–Ft. Worth Airport. Service began in 1974. The third GRT demonstration connected three separate campuses of West Virginia University at Morgantown. Boeing Aerospace Company became the manager of the project, which was largely based on a proposal by Alden Self-Transit Systems Corporation. Public service began in October 1975. The system was expanded with a UMTA grant and operations began in July 1979 (U.S. DOT, 1983b).

By the end of 1975 another 18 systems were in operation or under construction. They were all simple shuttle loop transit (SLT) systems at airports, amusement parks, and shopping centers. All were funded with private funds (U.S. DOT, 1983b).

In September 1974 the U.S. Senate Transportation Appropriations Committee directed the Congressional Office of Technology Assessment (OTA) to assess the potential for AGT systems. The report, produced in June 1975, was a comprehensive assessment of AGT systems and contained five reports from panels of specialists. Overall the report concluded that the $95 million spent on AGT research and development up to that time by UMTA had not produced the direct results expected in the form of fully developed systems in urban settings. The OTA went further in concluding that insufficient funding was directed at new systems research and that the program needed restructuring with a clarification of objectives (U.S. Congress, OTA, 1975).

The OTA found that SLT systems were promising for specialized urban transportation problems. With regard to the more sophisticated GRT systems, the OTA found that a number of cities had shown interest but that there were serious technical problems. As to the small vehicle personal rapid transit (PRT) systems, only preliminary studies were recommended. A major conclusion was that the program emphasized hardware development, but further research was needed on social, economic, and environmental impacts. Also UMTA had not developed a mechanism for qualifying new technological systems for capital grants (U.S. Congress, OTA, 1975).

In response to the study, UMTA launched the AGT Socio-Economic Research Program in 1976. It consisted of assessments of existing AGT installations, studies of capital and operating costs, travel market analyses, and an assessment of AGT technology compared with other alternatives in urban area application (U.S. DOT, 1983b).

A review of local planning studies conducted under this program found that more than 20 cities had considered AGT systems. The conclusion reached was that there was considerable uncertainty with regard to costs, public acceptance, reliability, crime, and land-use impacts (Lee, et al., 1978). Planning procedures and data were not available to adequately assess new technological systems as an alternative to conventional urban technologies.

Also in 1976, UMTA initiated the Downtown People Mover (DPM) program. It was designed to demonstrate the application of an SLT-type system in an urban environment. Impact studies were to be conducted to assess the systems with regard to patronage, community acceptance, reliability, maintainability, safety, and economics. Four cities were selected for these demonstrations: Cleveland, Houston, Los Angeles, and St. Paul. Three other cities were approved for participation using their existing commitments of federal funds: Detroit, Miami, and Baltimore (Mabee and Zumwalt, 1977). Detroit and Miami are currently constructing DPMs.

Policy on Major Urban Mass Transportation Investments

The level of federal funds for urban mass transportation had increased dramatically since 1970. However, the requests for federal funds from urban areas outpaced that increase. In particular there was a resurgence of the conviction that rail transit systems could largely solve the problems of congestion and petroleum dependence while promoting efficient development patterns. Consequently the need to assure that these funds were used effectively and productively became apparent.

The UMTA set forth its views on this issue in the document, *Preliminary Guidelines and Background Analysis* (Transportation Research Board, 1975a). It was prepared for review at a conference on the Evaluation of Urban Transportation Alternatives held at Airlie House, Virginia, in February 1975. The conference was attended by a broad spectrum of persons from all levels of government, the transit industry, consultants, universities, and private citizens. The conference report indicated a number of concerns with the guidelines, which were transmitted to the UMTA (Transportation Research Board, 1977).

With the assistance of the conference findings, the UMTA developed a draft policy statement to guide future decisions regarding federal assistance in the funding of major mass transportation projects. This *Proposed Policy on Major Urban Mass Transportation Investments* was published in August 1975 (U.S. DOT, 1975c). It embodied a number of principles.

First, area-wide transportation improvement plans should be multimodal and include region-wide and community-level transit services. Second, major mass transportation investment projects should be planned and implemented in stages to avoid premature investment in costly fixed facilities and to preserve maximum flexibility to respond to future unknowns. Third, full consideration should be given to improving the management and operation of existing transportation systems. Fourth, the analysis of alternatives should include a determination of which alternative meets the local area's social, environmental, and transportation goals in a cost effective manner. And fifth, full opportunity should be provided for involvement of the public and local officials in all phases of the planning and evaluation process (Transportation Research Board, 1977).

The UMTA stated that the level of federal funding would be based on a cost-effective alternative that would meet urban area needs and goals in a 5–15-year time frame and that was consistent with the long-range transportation plan.

A second Conference on Urban Transportation Alternative Analysis was held in March/April 1976 at Hunt Valley, Maryland. This conference, too, was attended by a broad spectrum of the professional community. There was considerable discussion on several issues including the criteria to be used to measure cost-effectiveness, where the cost-effectiveness analysis fit in the overall planning process, and the differences in the project development process between transit and highways (Transportation Research Board, 1977).

Using the recommendations from the second conference the UMTA prepared and published a final policy statement in September 1976 (U.S. DOT, 1976b). Although changes in the proposed policy were made, the principles remained basically unchanged.

In February 1978 the UMTA provided further elaboration in its Policy Toward Rail Transit. It stated that new rail transit lines or extensions would be funded in areas where population densities, travel volumes, and growth patterns indicated the need. Preference would be given to corridors serving densely populated urban centers. It reaffirmed the principles of analysis of alternatives, including TSM measures, incremental implementation, and cost-effectiveness. The policy added the requirement that the local area had to commit itself to a program of supportive actions designed to improve the cost-effectiveness, patronage, and prospect for economic viability of the investment. This included automobile management policies; feeder service; plans, policies and incentives to stimulate high density private development near stations; and other measures to revitalize nearby older neighborhoods and the central business district. With this policy supplement, rail transit was to become a tool for urban redevelopment.

Light Rail Transit

In the late 1960s and early 1970s, many urban areas were seeking alternatives to the construction of freeways. San Francisco and Washington, D.C. had decided to construct rail transit systems, but many areas did not have the density or potential travel demand to justify such systems. Moreover, rail transit systems had high construction costs and disrupted the areas through which they passed during construction. Busways and preferential treatment for buses were being considered as alternatives to high cost fixed guideway systems, particularly in the United States. In Europe, especially West Germany, light rail transit was the preferred alternative. This European experience renewed interest in light rail systems in the United States (Diamant, 1976).

In 1971 the San Francisco Municipal Railway (Muni) requested bids on 78 new light rail vehicles to replace its deteriorating PCC car fleet. The two bids that were received were rejected as being too costly. About this time, the Massachusetts Bay Transportation Authority (MBTA) and the Southeastern Pennsylvania Transportation Authority (SEPTA) decided to preserve and upgrade their light rail systems. These events provided the opportunity to develop a standard design for common use. The UMTA authorized a grant to the MBTA to develop specifications for a new U.S. Standard Light Rail Vehicle (SLRV). The first SLRVs were built by Boeing Vertol and tested in 1974 at the UMTA's test track in Pueblo, Colorado (Silien and Mora, 1975).

In December 1975 UMTA expressed its concern that urban areas should give adequate consideration to light rail transit (LRT) in a Policy Statement on Light Rail Transit. The UMTA stated that while it had no modal favorites, the increasing demand for transit capital assistance combined with escalating transit construction costs made it essential that cost effective approaches be fully explored. UMTA considered LRT as a potentially attractive option for many urban areas and would assist in its deployment in areas where proper conditions existed (Transportation Systems Center, 1977).

As interest in LRT grew, a series of conferences was organized to exchange information and explore the technical aspects and applications of LRT. The first conference, held in Philadelphia in 1975, had as its objective the reintroduction of LRT to a wide spectrum of decision makers in government, industry, and academia (Transportation Research Board, 1975b). In 1977 a second conference in Boston addressed the need for a more detailed focus on the theme of planning and technology (Transportation Research Board, 1978). Several years later, in 1982, a third conference occurred in San Diego with the theme of planning design, and implementation of LRT in existing urban environments (Transportation Research Board, 1982c). The fourth conference in Pittsburgh in 1985 focused on cost-effective approaches in the deployment of LRT systems that capitalized on the flexibility of this mode of transit (Transportation Research Board, 1985).

By 1985 LRT had achieved a substantial resurgence in the United States. Boston, Philadelphia, San Francisco, Pittsburgh, Cleveland, and Newark had renovated existing lines or replaced their existing vehicle fleets or both. Buffalo and San Diego had opened new LRT lines. And new LRT lines were under construction in Sacramento, Portland, Santa Clara, and Los Angeles.

Federal Aid Highway Act of 1976

The Federal Aid Highway Act of 1976 broadened the use of funds from trade-ins of nonessential Interstate routes. The process of increasing flexibility in the use of Interstate funds began with Section 103(e)(2), referred to as the Howard-Cramer Amendment, of the Federal Aid Highway Act of 1968. It allowed withdrawal of a nonessential Interstate route and the use of the funds on another Interstate route in the state.

In the Federal Aid Highway Act of 1973, Section 103(e)(4) allowed urbanized areas to withdraw a nonessential Interstate segment within an area upon joint request of local elected officials and the governor. An equivalent amount of funds could then be spent from general revenues for mass transportation capital projects at an 80 percent federal matching share. The 1976 act allowed the funds from the Interstate substitution to be used also for other highways and busways serving those urbanized areas (Bloch, et al., 1982).

The 1976 act also changed the definition of construction to allow federal funds to be expended on resurfacing, restoration, and rehabilitation (3R) of highways. This was done in recognition of the growing problem of highway deterioration. The completion date for the Interstate system was extended to September 30, 1990. Finally, the act expanded the transferability of federal funds among different federal-aid systems, thereby increasing flexibility in the use of these funds.

Urban System Study

The joint highway/transit planning regulations were controversial during their preparation and after their issuance. The states contended that the federal requirement to create metropolitan planning organizations (MPOs) with the responsibility to program funds preempted the states' right of self-determination. In essence they argued that MPOs were another level of government. Those at the local level of government were more supportive of the regulations, especially the greater authority to select projects and program funds. But there was widespread concern that the planning and programming process had become too inflexible and cumbersome (U.S. DOT, 1976a).

Consequently the Federal Aid Highway Act of 1976 required a study of the various factors involved in the planning, programming, and implementation of routes on the urban system. The study was conducted jointly by the FHWA and UMTA and submitted to Congress in January 1977 (U.S. DOT, 1976a). It was a major undertaking involving a liaison group of 12 organizations representing state and local interests, site visits to 30 urbanized areas, and field data on the remaining areas.

The study concluded that the planning requirements were being carried out responsibly by all participants. This was true in spite of the controversy over the responsibilities of the MPO. They also found that the flexibility in the use of urban system funds for transit was not widely used. Only 6.4 percent of the funds were being used for transit projects. It was concluded that overall the complexity of federal requirements deterred many local governments from using their federal urban system funds (Heanue, 1977). The study recommended that no changes should be made at that time, that the process was new and participants had not had sufficient time to adjust, and that even though there was some confusion and controversy, the process was working properly (U.S. DOT, 1976a).

Clean Air Act Amendments of 1977

The Clean Air Act Amendments of 1977 increased the flexibility and local responsibility in the administration of the Clean Air Act. The amendments required state and local governments to develop revisions to state implementation plans (SIPs) for all areas where the national ambient air quality standards had not been attained. The revised SIPs were to be submitted to the EPA by January 1, 1979, and approved by May 1, 1979.

The revised plans had to provide for attainment of national ambient air quality standards by 1982, or in the case of areas with severe photochemical oxidant or carbon monoxide problems, no later than 1987. In the latter case, a state must demonstrate that the standards cannot be met with all reasonable stationary and transportation control measures. The plans also had to provide for incremental reductions in emissions ("reasonable further progress") between the time the plans were submitted and the attainment deadline. If a state failed to submit a SIP or if EPA disapproved the SIP and the state failed to revise it in a satisfactory manner, EPA was required to promulgate regulations establishing a SIP by July 1, 1979. If, after July 1, 1979, EPA determined that a state was not fulfilling the requirements under the act, it was to impose sanctions. This would include stopping federal aid for highways (Cooper and Hidinger, 1980).

In many major urbanized areas the revised SIPs required the development of transportation control plans (TCPs) that included strategies to reduce emissions from transportation-related sources by means of structural or operational changes in the transportation system. Since state and local governments implement changes in the transportation system, the act strongly encouraged the preparation of transportation elements of the SIP by metropolitan planning organizations. These local planning organizations were responsible for developing the transportation control measure element of the SIPs (Cooper and Hidinger, 1980).

From 1978 to 1980, the DOT and EPA, after long negotiations, jointly issued several policy documents to implement the Clean Air Act's transportation requirements. One of these, signed in June 1978, was a "Memorandum of Understanding" that established the means by which the DOT and the EPA would assure the integration of transportation and air quality planning. A second one issued also in June 1978, "Transportation Air Quality Planning Guidelines" described the acceptable planning process to satisfy the requirements. Another, in March 1980, was a notice containing guidelines for receiving air quality planning grants under section 175 of the act (Cooper and Hidinger, 1980).

In January 1981 DOT issued regulations on air quality conformance and priority procedures for use in federal highway and transit programs. The regulations required that transportation plans, programs, and projects conform with the approved SIPs in areas that had not met ambient air quality standards, termed "nonattainment areas." In those areas, priority for transportation funds was to be given to "transportation control measures" (TCMs) that contributed to reducing air pollution emissions from transportation sources. Where an area's transportation plan or program was not in conformance with the TCM, "sanctions" were to be applied that prohibited the use of federal funds on major transportation projects (U.S. DOT, 1981b).

The 1977 Clean Air Act Amendments certainly gave impetus to short-range planning and transportation system management strategies. They also added a new dimension to the institutional and analytical complexity of the planning process.

Service and Methods Demonstrations Program

The focus in transportation planning and development was shifting to shorter-term, low-capital improvements in the early 1970s. Many of these improvements, which were grouped under the term "transportation system management" techniques, were only in the conceptual stage or in limited applications in the United States and other countries. There was a need to perform the final steps of evaluation and development, where necessary, to bring these new improvement strategies into operational practice.

The Service and Methods Demonstrations (SMD) Program was established in 1974 to promote the development, demonstration, evaluation, and widespread adoption of innovative transit services and transportation management techniques throughout the United States. The program focused on concepts that used existing technology to create improvements that require relatively low levels of capital investment and that can be implemented within a short time frame. The concepts were demonstrated in real-world operational environments and evaluated to determine their costs, impacts, and implementation characteristics. Evaluation findings were widely disseminated to transportation planners, policymakers, and transit operators (Spear, 1979).

The SMD Program began with six demonstrations involving specialized transportation for the elderly and handicapped, double-deck buses, and priority lanes for highway occupancy vehicles. By 1978 the program was sponsoring 59 ongoing demonstrations, evaluating 31 special case study projects, and had begun a cooperative program with the FHWA to evaluate another 17 projects in the National Ridesharing Demonstration Program.

Projects were divided into four program areas. First, under conventional service improvements, projects concentrated on improving productivity, reliability, and effectiveness with such techniques as priority treatment for buses and other high occupancy vehicles, route restructuring, auto restricted zones, and articulated buses. In the second category of pricing and service innovation were projects on fare payment strategies, fare integration, fare change strategies, service changes, and parking pricing. The third category of paratransit services contained projects on ridesharing, brokerage, and taxicabs. Fourth, transportation services for special user groups focused on accessible bus services, user-side subsidies, coordination of social service agency transportation and rural public transportation (Spear, 1981).

The Service and Methods Demonstration Program made a major contribution to the identification, evaluation, and dissemination of transportation system management techniques. This effort accelerated the introduction and adoption of innovative approaches to the provision of public transportation service. It also spurred experimentation with new public transportation service concepts by other agencies at the state and local levels.

9

URBAN ECONOMIC REVITALIZATION

In the mid 1970s the country was feeling the effects of structural changes in the economy, high unemployment, inflation, and rising energy prices. Many of the problems had been developing for a number of years. The economy was in a transition from a predominantly manufacturing base to one that had a larger share concentrated in service, communication, and high technology industries. Jobs in the manufacturing sector were declining and new jobs were growing in the new sectors of the economy. People were moving to those areas of the country where the new jobs were being created, especially the South and the West. The older urban areas in the Northeast and Midwest were being affected most severely by these changes. But older central cities in all sections of the country were in decline as jobs and people migrated first to the suburbs and then to the newer urban areas where the economies were growing.

These older communities and central cities were severely distressed economically and limited in their ability to address these problems themselves. It was recognized that the federal government had contributed to these problems with programs that had unintended consequences. However, many of the decisions that affected changes in urban areas were outside the control of even the federal government and often any level of government. The federal, state, and local levels of government would, therefore, have to cooperate among themselves and with the private sector in order to alleviate these problems.

1978 National Urban Policy Report

In Title VII of the Housing and Urban Development Act of 1970 the Congress required preparation of biennial reports on national growth and development. Congress recognized the need to analyze the many aspects of the nation's growth in a systematic manner with the objective of formulating a national urban growth policy. The first report, transmitted to Congress in 1972, discussed the broad subject of national growth, including both rural and urban areas (Domestic Council, 1972). The 1974 report focused on the dominant role of the private sector in determining growth and the ways in which the public and private sector could influence development patterns. The 1976 report discussed the decline of older Northeastern cities, the constraints of energy, environmental resources, and the need to conserve and rehabilitate existing housing and public facilities. (Domestic Council, 1976).

The National Urban Policy and New Community Development Act of 1977 amended the 1970 Act to designate the report the "National Urban Policy Report" rather than the more general "Report on Urban Growth" (Domestic Council, 1976). Less than a year later, on March 27, 1978, President Carter presented his Message to Congress on National Urban Policy. The policy was designed to build a new Partnership to Conserve America's Communities, involving all levels of government, the private sector, and neighborhood and voluntary organizations. It contained a number of proposals to improve existing programs and for new initiatives with the purpose of revitalizing distressed central cities and older suburbs (U.S. HUD, 1978b).

The President's Message was followed in August by the President's 1978 National Urban Policy Report (U.S. HUD, 1978b). Like its predecessors, the report discussed the demographic, social, and economic trends in the nation's urban areas. But it was the first report to recommend a national urban policy. The recommendations in the Report and the President's Message were developed by an inter-departmental committee called the Urban and Regional Policy Group. The Group worked for a year with extensive public involvement to formulate its analysis of the problems and recommendations (U.S. HUD, 1978a).

The urban policy consisted of nine objectives. The first urban policy objective was, "Encourage and support efforts to improve local planning and management capacity and the effectiveness of existing federal programs by coordinating these programs, simplifying planning requirements, reorienting resources, and reducing paperwork." Other objectives called for greater state, private sector, and voluntary involvement to assist urban areas. Several objectives related to fiscal relief for distressed communities and assistance to disadvantaged persons. The last objective was for an improved physical environment and reduced urban sprawl (U.S. HUD, 1978b).

A wide range of legislative and administrative actions were taken to implement the national urban policy (U.S. HUD, 1980). The DOT (FHWA and UMTA) issued guidance for evaluating the impact on urban centers of major transportation projects and investments. The guidance required an analysis of the impacts of improvements in highways and transit on central cities' development, tax base, employment, accessibility and environment. In addition, impacts on energy conservation, and on minorities and neighborhoods were to be analyzed. Furthermore, the guidance required that improvements to existing facilities be considered first, including the repair and rehabilitation of transportation facilities and TSM measures to increase the effectiveness of those facilities. In this manner, the guidance sought to assure that the new investments in transportation facilities would be cost-effective (U.S. DOT, 1979e).

The new national urban policy gave added impetus to the shift from constructing new facilities to managing, maintaining, and replacing existing facilities. It was rooted in the belief that mobility could be assured despite energy, environmental, and financial constraints. The key was to manage the use of the automobile in the city better. The challenge was for the urban transportation planning process to maintain and enhance mobility while meeting these other objectives (Heanue, 1980).

Surface Transportation Assistance Act of 1978

The Surface Transportation Assistance Act of 1978 was the first act that combined highway, public transportation, and highway safety authorizations in one piece of legislation. It provided $51.4 billion for the fiscal years 1979 through 1982, with $30.6 billion for highways, $13.6 billion for public transportation, and $7.2 billion for highway safety. It was the first time that authorizations for the highway program were made for a four-year period. Highway Trust Fund user charges were extended five years to 1984 and the fund itself to 1985.

Title I, the Federal-Aid Highway Act of 1978, accelerated completion of the National System of Interstate and Defense Highways. It concentrated funds on projects that were ready to be constructed by changing the availability of a state's apportionment from four to two years. If the funds were not used, they could be reallocated to states with projects ready to go. The Act withdrew authority to replace one Interstate route with another. It placed a deadline of September 30, 1983, on substituting public transportation or other highway projects for withdrawn Interstate routes. The federal share for both highway and transit substitute projects was increased to 85 percent. The act required that environmental impact statements for Interstate projects be submitted by September 30, 1983, and that they be under contract or construction by September 30, 1986, if sufficient federal funds were available. If the deadlines were not met, the Interstate route or substitute project was to be eliminated.

The act also raised the federal share for non-Interstate highways from 70 to 75 percent. It further increased the allowable amount of funds that could be transferred among federal-aid systems to 50 percent. The eligibility of federal funds for carpools and vanpools was made permanent. The amount of $20 million annually for fiscal years 1979 through 1982 was authorized for bicycle projects. The act substantially increased the funding for bridge replacement and rehabilitation to $1 billion annually.

Title III, the Federal Public Transportation Act of 1978, expanded the Section 5 Formula Grant program. The basic program of operating and capital assistance was retained with the same population and population density formula at higher authorization levels. A "second tier" program was authorized with the same project eligibility and apportionment formula. However, the funds were to be initially split so that 85 percent went to urbanized areas over 750,000 in population and the remaining 15 percent to smaller areas. A third tier was established for routine purchases of buses and related facilities and equipment. A new fourth tier replaced the Section 17 and 18 commuter rail programs. The funds could be used for commuter rail or rail transit capital or operating expenses. The funds were apportioned two-thirds based on commuter rail vehicle miles and route miles and one-third on rail transit route miles.

The act changed the availability of funds for transit from two to four years. It formalized the "letter of intent" process whereby the federal government committed funds for a transit project in the Section 3 Discretionary Grant program. Public hearings were required for all general increases in fares or substantial changes in service. A small formula grant program for non-urbanized areas (Section 18) was established for capital and operating assistance. Apportioned on non-urbanized area population, it authorized an 80 percent federal share for capital projects and 50 percent for operating assistance. The act also established an intercity bus terminal development program, intercity bus service operating subsidy program, and human resources program for urban transit systems.

The urban transportation planning requirement was changed in an identical fashion in the highway and transit titles. Energy conservation was included as a new goal in the planning process and alternative transportation system management strategies were required to be evaluated. The designation of Metropolitan Planning Organizations was to be by agreement among general purpose units of local government and in cooperation the governor. For the transit program, it was further required that plans and programs encourage to the maximum extent feasible the participation of private enterprise. Funding for transit planning grants was set at 5.5 percent of Section 3 appropriations.

A "Buy American" provision was included to apply to all contracts over $500,000. The provision could be waived if: its application was inconsistent with the public interest; domestic supplies were not available or of unsatisfactory quality; or if the use of domestic products would increase the cost by over 10 percent.

National Energy Act of 1978

In 1979 Iran cut off crude oil shipments to Western nations, causing shortages of oil products, especially gasoline, and price increases. Most of the regulations implemented in 1973 and 1974 were still in effect and basically unchanged. (Diesel fuel prices had been deregulated in 1976.) During the intervening years, other legislation had been passed to stimulate oil production and foster conservation (Schueftan and Ellis, 1981). The Department of Energy Organization Act of 1977 brought together most federal energy functions under a single cabinet level department.

In October 1978 the Congress passed the National Energy Act, which was composed of five bills. The National Energy Conservation Policy Act of 1978 extended two energy conservation programs that required states to undertake specific conservation actions including the promotion of carpools and vanpools. The Powerplant and Industrial Fuel Use Act of 1978 required Federal agencies to conserve natural gas and petroleum in programs which they administered (U.S. Dept. of Energy, 1978). To implement Section 403(b) of the act, President Carter signed Executive Order 12185 in December 1979 extending existing efforts to promote energy conservation through federal-aid programs.

The DOT issued final regulations in August 1980 in compliance with the Executive Order. These regulations required that all phases of transportation projects from planning to construction and operations be conducted in a manner that conserves fuel. It incorporated energy conservation as a goal into the urban transportation planning process and required an analysis of alternative TSM improvements to reduce energy consumption (U.S. DOT, 1980c).

Other actions affected urban transportation and planning. President Carter signed an Executive Order in April 1979 that began the phased decontrol of petroleum prices. By September 30, 1981, petroleum prices were to be determined completely by the free market. This process was accelerated by President Reagan through an Executive Order in January 1981, which immediately terminated all price and allocation controls (Cabot Consulting Group, 1982).

The Emergency Energy Conservation Act of 1979, which was signed in November 1979, required the President to establish national and state conservation targets. States were to submit emergency conservation plans that would meet the targets. The act expired in July 1983 without targets being set nor plans prepared. However, many states became active in contingency planning for a potential future energy emergency (Cabot Consulting Group, 1982).

Energy conservation had become integrated into the urban transportation planning process as a result of federal and state legislation and regulation. It gave further impetus to reducing the use of automobiles and for emphasis on transportation system management. Energy contingency planning became more widespread by planning organizations, transit authorities, and highway departments.

BART Impact Program

The San Francisco Bay Area Rapid Transit (BART) system was the first regional rail transit system to be built in the U.S. since World War II. It provided a unique opportunity for studying the impacts of such a system on the urban environment. The BART Impact Program was organized to evaluate the effects of BART on the economy, environment, and people of the Bay Area. It began in 1972 with the start of BART system operation and lasted six years.

The study addressed a broad range of potential rail transit impacts, including impacts on the transportation system and travel behavior, land use and urban development, the environment, public policy, the regional economy, and social institutions and lifestyles. The incidence of these impacts on population groups, local areas, and economic sectors was also measured and analyzed. (Metropolitan Transportation Commission, 1979a, 1979b).

The BART system included 71 miles of track with 34 stations of which 23 had parking lots (Fig. 9.1). The four lines had stations spaced one-third to one-half mile apart in the cities of San Francisco and Oakland, and two to four miles apart in the suburbs. In 1975 BART served a population of about 1 million persons residing in three counties. Fares range from $0.25 to $1.45, with discounts for the elderly, handicapped, and children. BART cost $1.6 billion to build of which 80 percent was locally funded (Metropolitan Transportation Commission, 1979a, 1979b).

The program produced a considerable amount of information on the impacts of BART and, by implication the impacts of rail systems on urban areas. Its major findings included:

- BART provided a significant increase in the capacities of the major regional travel corridors, particularly approaching the cities of San Francisco and Oakland. However, it had not provided a long-term solution for traffic congestion because the additional capacity had been filled by new trips that had previously been deterred by traffic congestion. It most effectively served suburbanites commuting to work in San Francisco.
- BART had been integrated into the Bay Area with a minimum of environmental and social disruption because of its careful planning and design.
- To date, BART had not had a major impact on Bay Area land use. Some land use changes were evident where BART provided travel time advantages, where communities had acted to support and enhance the system's impacts through zoning and development plans, and where market demand for new development was strong, as in downtown San Francisco. It was likely that many potential impacts had not yet had time to develop.
- The $1.2 billion expended in the Bay Area for BART construction generated local expenditures totalling $3.1 billion during a twelve-year period. However, over the long term, BART had not induced economic growth in the Bay Area; that is, the system had not measurably enhanced the competitive advantage of the region in relation to other metropolitan areas in the country. (Metropolitan Transportation Commission, 1979a, 1979b)

An important implication of the BART Impact Program's findings was that by itself rail transit could be expected to have only a limited impact on the various aspects of the urban environment. Existing local conditions and the enactment of supportive policies were more important in determining the influence of a rail system on an urban area. For example, neither BART nor any other similar rail system was likely to cause high density residential development nor discourage urban sprawl in an established urban area unless strong regionally coordinated land use controls were implemented.

FIGURE 9.1. The BART system

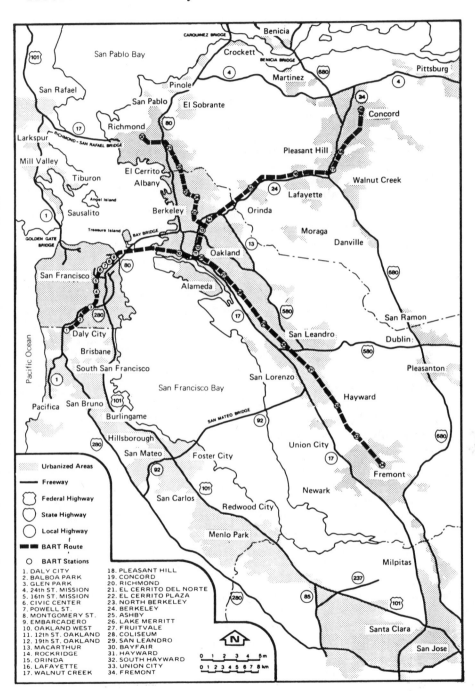

Partly as a result of the BART experience, the Urban Mass Transportation Administration began to require localities building or planning to build new rail lines with federal assistance to commit themselves to a program of local supportive actions to enhance the project's cost effectiveness and patronage.

Council on Environmental Quality's Regulations

The Council on Environmental Quality (CEQ) issued final regulations on November 29, 1978, establishing uniform procedures for implementing the procedural provisions of the National Environmental Policy Act of 1969. They applied to all federal agencies and took effect on July 30, 1979. They were issued because the 1973 CEQ Guidelines for preparing environmental impact statements (EISs) were not viewed consistently by all agencies, leading to differences in interpretations (CEQ, 1978).

The regulations embodied several new concepts designed to make the EIS more useful to decision makers and the public, and to reduce paperwork and delays. First, the regulations created a "scoping" process to provide for the early identification of significant impacts and issues. It also provided for allocating responsibility for the EIS among the lead agency and cooperating agencies. The scoping process was to be integrated with other planning activities (CEQ, 1978).

Second, the regulations permitted "tiering" of the EIS process. This provided that environmental analyses completed at a broad scale (for example, region) need not be duplicated for site-specific projects; the broader analyses could be summarized and incorporated by reference. The purpose of "tiering" was to eliminate repetition and allow discussion of issues at the appropriate level of detail (CEQ, 1978).

Third, in addition to the previously required EIS, which discussed the alternatives being considered, a "record of decision" document was required. It had to identify the "environmentally preferable" alternative, the other alternatives considered, and the factors used in reaching the decision. Until this document was issued, no action could be taken on an alternative that would adversely affect the environment or limit the choice of alternatives (CEQ, 1978).

The regulations generally sought to reduce the paperwork in the EIS process by such techniques as limiting the length of the document to 150 pages (300 in complex situations), specifying a standard format, emphasizing that the process focus on real alternatives, allowing incorporation of material by reference, and by using summaries for circulation instead of the entire EIS. Agencies were encouraged to set time limits on the process and to integrate other statutory and analysis requirements into a single process.

In October 1980 the FHWA and UMTA published supplemental implementing procedures. They established a single set of environmental procedures for highway and urban transit projects. They also integrated the UMTA's procedures for alternatives analysis under its major investment policy with the new EIS procedures. This permitted the preparation of a single draft EIS/alternatives analysis document. These regulations were an important step toward integrating highway and transit planning and reducing duplicative documentation (U.S. DOT, 1980b).

International Conferences on Behavioral Travel Demand

The Williamsburg Urban Travel Forecasting Conference gave widespread recognition to disaggregate behavioral demand models. The momentum created by this conference caused an upsurge in research in behavioral travel demand. The research was so extensive and widespread that the need arose for better interchange of ideas and developments.

To fill this void, the Transportation Research Board Committee on Traveler Behavior and Values organized a series of four International Conferences on Behavioral Travel Demand. The conferences were held every two years: South Berwick, Maine, in 1973 (Stopher and Meyburg, 1974); Asheville, North Carolina, in 1975 (Stopher and Meyburg, 1976); Melbourne, Australia, in 1977 (Hensher and Stopher, 1979); and Grainau, Germany, in 1979 (Stopher, Meyburg, and Brog, 1981).

The proceedings of these conferences provide a comprehensive documentation of the progress in behavioral travel demand research and the important issues concerning the research community. Research recommendations often served as the agenda for further work in the following years. The focus of these discussions was to gain a better understanding of travel behavior and to develop travel demand models with stronger theoretical bases. Using this approach, travel forecasting would become more sensitive to relevant policy issues, require less data to estimate, and be less costly and time-consuming to use.

Great strides were made in achieving these ends. But in doing so, a class of models was produced that was substantially different from conventional forecasting techniques. As a result, progress in diffusing these techniques into practice was slow. This issue then became major concern in the field of travel forecasting.

Urban Initiatives Program

The National Mass Transportation Assistance Act of 1974 authorized the use of federal funds for joint development purposes through the Young Amendment. The Young Amendment allowed local agencies to use federal funds to improve those facilities within the zone affected by the construction and operation of mass transit improvements that were needed to be compatible with land-use patterns. Assistance was available for establishing public or quasi-public corridor development corporations (Gortmaker, 1980).

The Urban Initiatives program, however, was not implemented until it was authorized in Section 3(a) (1) (D) of the Surface Transportation Assistance Act of 1978. This section of the Act authorized federal grants for land acquisition and the provision of utilities on land that was physically or functionally related to transit facilities for the purpose of stimulating economic development.

The Urban Initiatives program was one element of the DOT effort to implement President Carter's Urban Policy. The guidelines for the program were issued in April 1979. The program allowed expenditures for preconstruction activities (e.g., design and engineering studies, land acquisition and write-down, and real estate packaging) and items that connect transportation with land developments (e.g., pedestrian connections, parking, and street furniture). Preference was to be given to projects that demonstrated that they advanced Urban Policy objectives.

During the three years of the program, 46 projects were funded in 43 urban areas. They integrated transportation projects with economic development activities. Many of these projects were transit malls or intermodal terminals. The program extended the traditional funding beyond direct transit projects to the related development tied to transit service (Rice Center, 1981).

The practice of setting aside federal funds for Urban Initiatives' projects was discontinued in March 1981. However, these types of activities continued to be eligible for funding under the regular transit programs.

Section 504 Regulations on Accessibility for the Handicapped

Section 504 of the Rehabilitation Act of 1973 provided that no person who is otherwise qualified should be discriminated against due to handicap in any program or activity receiving federal financial assistance. In 1976 the UMTA issued regulations that required "special efforts" in planning public mass transportation facilities that can be utilized by elderly and handicapped persons. It also required that new transit vehicles and facilities be accessible to the handicapped. Handicapped groups thought the regulations were too vague and difficult to enforce (U.S. DOT, 1976c).

More stringent regulations were published in May 1979. It required all existing bus and rail systems to become fully accessible to handicapped persons within three years. This included fifty percent of the buses in fixed route service to be accessible to wheelchair users. For extraordinarily expensive facilities, the time limit could be extended to 10 years for bus facilities, to 30 years for rail facilities, and to 5 years for rail cars. Steady progress to achieve accessibility was required. New facilities and equipment were still required to be accessible to receive federal assistance (U.S. DOT, 1979f).

Transit authorities complained that the requirements were far too costly and sued the DOT for exceeding its authority. The U.S. Court of Appeals in a decision in 1981 said that the 1979 regulations went beyond the DOT's authority under Section 504. Following the decision, the DOT issued regulations on an interim basis and indicated that there would be new rulemaking leading to a final rule. The interim regulations required applicants to certify that "special efforts" were being made to provide transportation that was accessible to handicapped persons (U.S. DOT, 1981a).

Section 317(c) of the Surface Transportation Assistance Act of 1982 required the DOT to publish a proposed rule that would include (1) minimum criteria for the provision of transportation services to handicapped and elderly individuals, (2) a public participation mechanism, and (3) procedures for the UMTA to monitor transit authorities' performance.

The DOT's regulations for how transit authorities should carry out the Section 504 had long been controversial. The DOT has had a difficult job accommodating both the concerns of the handicapped community for adequate public transportation and the concerns of transit authorities and local governments for avoiding costly or rigid requirements. This rulemaking process has been one of the most complex and protracted in urban transportation. It has engendered a fierce debate between those who felt that handicapped persons should have the right to be mainstreamed into society and those who believed that there were more cost-effective means of providing transportation for those persons using paratransit-type services. This full accessibility versus equal service debate is not over. The DOT's new regulations will seek to find a middle ground between the two points of view.

Aspen Conference on Future Urban Transportation

As the decade drew to a close, the assault on the automobile never seemed so widespread. Energy conservation and environmental protection were national priorities. Fiscal resources were constrained and cost-effectiveness was the major criterion in urban transportation evaluations. Reversing central city decline was emerging as a key concern. And mobility for the transportation disadvantaged still required attention (Hassell, 1982). What was the future for urban personal mobility in the United States? Had the dominance of the automobile in the U.S. economy and society peaked?

To address these issues, the Transportation Planning Division of the American Planning Association sponsored the Aspen Conference on Future Urban Transportation in June 1979. The conference was supported and attended by representatives of both the public and private sector. The conferees could not reach a consensus on an image of the future but agreed on a range of factors that would be influential. Incremental planning was seen as the only feasible and desirable approach to the future (American Planning Assoc., 1979).

The conferees did conclude that there are "...no panaceas; no substantial increases in mobility due to new techniques...no quick or cheap energy solutions, and none without major environmental risks and costs...no promise of breakthrough in environmental technology...no major solutions through changes in living patterns or economic structure...no simple mechanism for restructuring urban form so as to reduce urban travel...." (American Planning Assoc., 1979). The conferees did make certain general recommendations for approaches to energy, mobility and accessibility, environmental, social, safety, and economic issues. They concluded that, at least for the balance of this century, the automobile would continue to be the principal and preferred mode of urban transportation for the majority of the American people. Public transportation would become increasingly important in supplying mobility. Both would require increased public investment from all levels of government (American Planning Assoc., 1979).

10

DECENTRALIZATION OF DECISION MAKING

Through the decade of the 1970s there was a sharp increase in the range and complexity of issues required to be addressed in the urban transportation planning process. The combination of requirements and regulations had become burdensome and counter-productive. Organizations and techniques seemed unable to adapt with sufficient speed. It was becoming impossible to analyze all of the tradeoffs that were required. This problem was not confined to urban transportation but to most activities where the federal government was involved. It ushered in a new mood in the nation to decentralize control and authority, and to reduce federal intrusion into local decision making (Weiner, 1983).

President Reagan's Memorandum on Regulations

On January 29, 1981, President Reagan sent a memorandum to all major domestic agencies to postpone the implementation of all regulations that were to take effect within the coming 60 days (Reagan, 1981b). This was to provide time for the newly appointed Task Force on Regulatory Relief to develop regulatory review procedures.

The Executive Order 12291 on Federal Regulation was issued on February 17, 1981 (Reagan, 1981a). It established procedures for reviewing existing regulations and evaluating new ones. It required that a regulation have greater benefits to society than costs and that the approach used must maximize those benefits. All regulatory actions were to be based on a regulatory impact analysis that assessed the benefits and costs.

The order set in motion a major effort at the federal level to eliminate and simplify regulations and limit the issuance of new regulations. The impact on federal agencies was quickly felt.

Airlie House Conference on Urban
Transportation Planning in the 1980s

Concern had been growing in the planning community about the future of urban transportation planning. On the one hand planning requirements had become more complex, new planning techniques had not found their way into practice, and future changes in social, demographic, energy, environmental, and technological factors were unclear. On the other hand, fiscal constraints were tight and the federal government was shifting the burden of decision making to state and local governments and the private sector. The future of planning was in doubt.

To address these concerns, a conference was held at Airlie House, in Virginia, on November 9–12, 1981, on Urban Transportation Planning in the 1980s. The conference reaffirmed the need for systematic urban transportation planning, especially to maximize the effectiveness of limited public funds. But the planning process needed to be adjusted to the nature and scope of area problems. It might not be the same for growing and for declining areas, nor for corridor- and for regional-level problems (Transportation Research Board, 1982b).

The conferees also concluded that the federal government had been overly restrictive in its regulations, making the planning process costly, time-consuming, and difficult to administer. It was concluded that the regulations should be streamlined, specifying goals to be achieved and leaving the decisions on how to meet them to the states and local governments. The conferees called for a recognition of the need for different levels of 3C planning by urbanized areas of various sizes. Additionally, greater flexibility in the requirements for MPOs was recommended, with more responsibility given to the agencies that implement transportation projects; and finally, less frequent federal certification was recommended (Transportation Research Board, 1982b).

Increased attention to system management and fiscal issues was needed, but long-range planning needed also to identify shifts in the major longer-term trends that would affect the future of urban areas. This strategic planning process should be flexible to fit local concerns (Transportation Research Board, 1982b).

The conference recommendations reflected the new mood that the federal government had over-regulated and was too specific in its requirements. The planning process was straining under this burden, finding it difficult to plan to meet local needs. The burden had to be lifted for the planning process to be viable.

Federal Aid Highway Act of 1981

The Federal Aid Highway Act of 1981 established early completion and preservation of the Interstate system as the highest priority highway program. To ensure early completion, the act reduced the cost to complete the system by nearly $14 billion, from $53 billion to $39 billion, by limiting eligible construction items to those that provided a minimum level of acceptable service. This included: full access control; a pavement design to accommodate twenty year forecasted travel; meeting essential environmental requirements; a maximum design of six lanes in areas under 400,000 in population and eight lanes in larger areas; and, any high occupancy lanes previously approved in the 1981 Interstate Cost Estimate (ICE).

The act expanded the Interstate resurfacing, restoration, and rehabilitation (3R) program by added reconstruction as an eligible category. This new category of the new 4R program included the addition of travel lanes, construction and reconstruction of interchanges, and the acquisition of right-of-way. Construction items that were removed from the Interstate construction program were eligible for 4R funding. The federal share was increased from 75 percent under the 3R program to 90 percent under the 4R program. Funds were to be allocated to states based 55 percent on Interstate lane miles and 45 percent on vehicle miles of travel. Every state with Interstate mileage had to receive a minimum of 0.5 percent of the funds for the program.

This act marked a shift in focus in the federal highway program toward finally completing the Interstate system and moving ahead with rehabilitating it.

Executive Order 12372

Office of Management and Budget's Circular A-95 (which replaced Bureau of the Budget Circular A-95) had governed the consultation process on federal grant programs with state and local governments since its issuance in July 1969. Although the A-95 process had served a useful function in assuring intergovernmental cooperation on federal grant programs, there were concerns that the process had become too rigid and cumbersome and caused unnecessary paperwork. To respond to these concerns and to delegate more responsibility and authority to state and local governments, the President signed Executive Order 12372, "Intergovernmental Review of Federal Programs," on July 14, 1982 (Reagan, 1982).

The objectives of the Executive Order were to foster an intergovernmental partnership and strengthen federalism by relying on state and local processes for intergovernmental coordination and review of federal financial assistance and direct federal development. The Executive Order had several purposes. First, it allowed states, after consultation with local officials, to establish their own process for review and comment on proposed federal financial assistance and direct federal development. Second, it increased federal responsiveness to state and local officials by requiring federal agencies to "accommodate" or "explain" when considering certain state and local views. Third, it allowed states to simplify, consolidate, or substitute state plans. The order also revoked OMB Circular A-95, although regulations implementing this Circular remained in affect until September 30, 1983.

There were three major elements that comprised the process under the Executive Order. These were: establishing a state process, the single point of contact, and the federal agency's "accommodate" or "explain" response to state and local comments submitted in the form of a recommendation. First, a state could choose which programs and activities are being included under that state process after consulting with local governments. The elements of the process were to be determined by the state. A state was not required to establish a state process; however, if no process was established, the provisions of the Executive Order did not apply. Existing consultation requirements of other statutes or regulations would continue in effect, including those of the Intergovernmental Cooperation Act of 1968 and the Demonstration Cities and Metropolitan Development Act of 1966.

Second, a single point of contact had to be designated by the state for dealing with the federal government. The single point of contact was the only official contact for state and local views to be sent to the federal government and to receive the response.

Third, when a single point of contact transmitted a state process recommendation, the federal agency receiving the recommendation had to either: (1) accept the recommendation ("accommodate"); (2) reach a mutually agreeable solution with the parties preparing the recommendation; or (3) provide the single point of contact with a written explanation for not accepting the recommendation or reaching a mutually agreeable solution. If there was nonaccommodation, the Department was generally required to wait 15 days after sending an explanation of the nonaccommodation to the single point of contact before taking final action.

The regulations implementing Executive Order 12372 for transportation programs were published on June 24, 1983 (U.S. DOT, 1983a). They applied to all federal-aid highway and urban public transportation programs.

Woods Hole Conference on Future
Directions of Urban Public Transportation

The transit industry was growing restless as the demands for and requirements on transit services were changing. Older cities were concerned about rehabilitation while newer ones were focused on expansion. Future changes in the economic base, land use, energy and sociodemographic characteristics were uncertain. The transit industry was coming out of a period where federal priorities and requirements had changed too frequently. Transit deficits had risen sharply over the previous decade and the federal government had declared that it planned to phase out operating subsidies. And many were calling for the private sector to provide an increased share of transit services because they were more efficient.

A diverse group of conferees met at the Woods Hole Study Center in Massachusetts, September 26–29, 1982, to discuss Future Directions of Urban Public Transportation (Transportation Research Board, 1984a). The conference addressed the role of public transportation, present and future, the context within which public transportation functioned, and strategies for the future. Attendees included leaders of the transit industry and government, academics, researchers, and consultants. There were wide differences of opinion that had not disappeared when the conference concluded.

The conferees did agree that "Strategic planning for public transportation should be conducted at both the local and national levels." The transit industry should be more aggressive in working with developers and local governments in growing parts of metropolitan areas to capitalize on opportunities to integrate transit facilities into major new developments. The industry needed to improve its relationship with highway and public works agencies as well as state and local decision makers. Financing transit had become more complex and difficult but had created new opportunities (Transportation Research Board, 1984a).

The conferees called for reductions in federal requirements and avoidance of rapid shifts in policy in the future. The federal government should have a more positive federal urban policy and the UMTA should be transit's advocate within the federal government (Transportation Research Board, 1984a).

Agreement could not be reached on the future role of urban transit. Some felt that the transit industry should only concern itself with conventional rail and bus systems. Others argued that transit agencies should broaden the range of services provided to include various forms of paratransit and ridesharing so as to attract a larger share of the travel market. Nevertheless, the conference was considered to be a first small step in a strategic planning process for the transit industry.

Easton Conference on Travel Analysis Methods for the 1980s

The Airlie House Conference on Urban Transportation Planning in the 1980s highlighted the shifts in planning that were occurring and were likely to continue (Transportation Research Board, 1982b). State and local governments would assume a greater role as the federal government disengaged, finances would be tighter, system rehabilitation would become more important, and traffic growth would be slower.

A conference was held at Easton, Maryland, in November 1982 to discuss how well travel analysis methods were adapted to the issues and problems of the 1980s. This Conference on Travel Analysis Methods for the 1980s focused on defining the state of the art versus the state of practice, describing how the methods have been and can be applied, and identifying gaps between art and practice that needed more dissemination of current knowledge, research, or development. The conference extended the discussions of the International Travel Demand Conferences but concentrated on the application of travel analysis methods and on improving the interaction between researchers and practitioners (Transportation Research Board, 1984b).

The conference reviewed the states of the art and practice and how they applied to the various levels of planning. There were extensive discussions on how capable travel analysis procedures were in dealing with major transportation issues and why they were not being extensively applied in practice (Transportation Research Board, 1984b).

The conferees found that in an era of scarce resources, sound analysis of alternatives would continue to be important. Travel analysis methods that were currently available were suitable for issues that could be foreseen in the 1980s. These disaggregate techniques, which had been developed during the 1970s, had been tested in limited applications and were now ready for widescale use. Their use in the analysis of small-scale projects, however, might not be justified because of their complexity (Transportation Research Board, 1984b).

It was clear, however, that new disaggregate travel analysis techniques were not being used extensively in practice. The gap between research and practice was wider than it had ever been. The new mathematical techniques and theoretical bases from econometrics and psychometrics had been difficult for practitioners to learn. Moreover, the new techniques were not easily integrated into conventional planning practices. Neither researchers nor practitioners had made the necessary effort to bridge the gap. Researchers had been unwilling to package and disseminate the new travel analysis methods in a form usable to practitioners. Practitioners had been unwilling to undergo retraining to be able to use these new techniques. Neither group had subjected these methods to rigorous tests to determine how well they performed or for what problems they were best suited (Transportation Research Board, 1984b).

The conferees concluded that the travel demand community should concentrate on transferring the new travel analysis methods into practice. A wide range of technology transfer approaches was suggested. The federal government and Transportation Research Board were recommended to lead in this endeavor (Transportation Research Board, 1984b).

Surface Transportation Assistance Act of 1982

Through the decade of the 1970s there was mounting evidence of deterioration in the nation's highway and transit infrastructure. Money during that period had been concentrated on building new capacity and the transition to funding rehabilitation of the infrastructure had been slow. By the time the problem was faced, the cost estimate to refurbish the highways, bridges, and transit systems had reached hundreds of billions of dollars (Weiner, 1983).

The Surface Transportation Assistance Act of 1982 was passed to address the infrastructure problem. The act extended authorizations for the highway and transit programs by four years, from 1983 to 1986. (See Table 10.1.) In addi-

TABLE 10.1. Surface Transportation Assistance Act of 1982

	Authorization Levels by Fiscal Year ($ Millions)			
	1983	1984	1985	1986
Highway Programs				
Interstate Construction	4,000.0	4,000.0	4,000.0	4,000.0
Interstate Rehabilitation	1,950.0	2,400.0	2,800.0	3,150.0
Interstate Highway Substitutions	257.0	700.0	700.0	725.0
Primary System	1,883.4	2,147.2	2,351.8	2,505.1
Secondary System	650.0	650.0	650.0	650.0
Urban System	800.0	800.0	800.0	800.0
Bridge Replacement & Rehabilitation	1,600.0	1,650.0	1,750.0	2,050.0
Safety Construction	390.0	390.0	390.0	390.0
Other Highway Programs	1,183.6	1,120.0	1,154.0	1,106.0
Subtotal, Highway	12,714.0	13,857.2	14,595.8	15,376.1
Urban Transit Programs				
Discretionary Capital Grants	779.0	1,250.0	1,100.0	1,100.0
Formula Grants	—	2,750.0	2,950.0	3,050.0
Interstate Transit Substitutions	365.0	380.0	390.0	400.0
R&D, Admin., & Misc.	86.3	91.0	100.0	100.0
Subtotal, Urban Transit	1,230.3	4,471.0	4,540.0	4,650.0
Total, Highway & Urban Transit	13,944.3	18,328.2	19,135.8	20,026.1

tion, the act raised the highway user charges by five cents (in addition to the existing four cents) a gallon on fuel effective April 1, 1983. Other taxes were changed including a substantial increase in the truck user fees, which were changed from a fixed rate to a graduated rate by weight. Of the revenues raised from the five cent increase in user fees (about $5.5 billion annually), the equivalent of a four cent raise in fuel user charges was to increase highway programs, and the remaining one cent was for transit programs (Weiner, 1983).

The additional highway funds were for accelerating completion of the Interstate highway system (to be completed by 1991), an increased 4R (Interstate resurfacing, restoration, rehabilitation, and reconstruction) program, a substantially expanded bridge replacement and rehabilitation program, and greater funding for Primary, Secondary, and Interstate projects (Weiner, 1983).

The act authorized the administration of highway planning and research (HP&R) funds as a single fund and made them available to the states for a four year period. A standard federal matching ratio for the HP&R program was set at 85 percent. A 1.5 percent share of bridge funds was authorized for HP&R purposes. As a result of the large expansion in the construction program, the level of funding increased substantially for the HP&R program and urban transportation planning (PL) purposes.

The act restructured federal urban transit programs. No new authorizations were made for the Section 5 formula grant program. Instead, a new formula grant program was created that allowed expenditures on planning, capital and operating items. Substantial discretion was given to state and local governments in selecting projects to be funded using formula grants with minimal federal interference. However, there were limitations on the use of the funds for operating expenses. The act provided for a distribution of funds into areas of different sizes by population; over one million, between one million and 200,000, under 200,000 and rural. Within these population groups, the funds were to be apportioned by several formulas using such factors as population density, vehicle miles, and route miles (Weiner, 1983).

The revenue from the one cent increase in highway user charges was to be placed into a Mass Transit Account of the Highway Trust Fund. The funds could only be used for capital projects. They were to be allocated by a formula in fiscal year 1983, but were discretionary in later years. The definition of capital was changed to include associated capital maintenance items. The act also provided that a substantial number of federal requirements be self-certified by the applicants and that other requirements be consolidated to reduce paperwork (Weiner, 1983).

A requirement was also included for a biennial report on transit performance and needs, with the first report due in January 1984. In addition the act provided that regulations be published that set minimum criteria on transportation services for the handicapped and elderly.

The Surface Transportation Assistance Act of 1982 was passed under considerable controversy about the future federal role in transportation, particularly the Administration's position to phase-out of federal transit operating subsidies. Debates on later appropriations bills demonstrated that the issue remained unresolved.

Advent of Microcomputers

By the early 1980s there was a surge in interest and use of microcomputers in urban transportation planning. The FHWA and UMTA had increasingly focused their computer related research and development activities on the application of small computers. These technical support activities were directed at gaining a better understanding of the potential and applicability of microcomputers, promoting the development and exchange of information and programs, and evaluating and testing programs. Some software development was carried out, but most software was produced commercially.

A user support structure was developed to assist state and local agencies. This included the establishment of two user support centers; one at Rensselear

Polytechnic Institute for the transit industry and a second at the DOT's Transportation Systems Center (TSC) for transportation planning, transportation system management (TSM), and traffic engineering applications. Three user groups were formed under DOT sponsorship; transit operations, transportation planning and TSM, and traffic engineering. These groups exchanged information and software, developed and promoted standards, and identified research and development needs. Assistance was provided through the user support centers. A newsletter, *MicroScoop*, was published periodically to aid in the communication process.

The FHWA and UMTA developed a one-day seminar entitled, "Microcomputers for Transportation" to acquaint users with the capabilities and uses of microcomputers. They also published reports on available software and sources of information (U.S. DOT, 1983d, 1983e). As the capabilities of microcomputers have increased, they have offered the opportunity of greater analytical capacity to a larger number of organizations; as a result, their use has become more widespread.

New Urban Transportation Planning Regulations

The joint FHWA/UMTA urban transportation planning regulations had served as the key federal guidance since 1975 (U.S. DOT, 1975a). During 1980 there was an intensive effort to amend these regulations to ensure more citizen involvement, to increase the emphasis on urban revitalization, and to integrate corridor planning into the urban transportation planning process (Paparella, 1982). Proposed amendments were published in October 1980. Final amendments were published in January 1981, to take effect in February.

These amendments were postponed as a result of President Reagan's January 1981 memorandum to delay the effective day of all pending regulations by 60 days. During this period the amendments were reviewed, based on the criteria in the President's memorandum and Executive Order 12291. Consequently the amendments were withdrawn and interim final regulations were issued in August 1981. These regulations included minimal changes to streamline the planning process in areas under 200,000 in population, to clarify transportation system management, and to incorporate legislative changes (U.S. DOT, 1983c).

To obtain public comment on further changes in the regulations, the FHWA and UMTA published an issues-and-options paper in December 1981, entitled Solicitation of Public Comment on the Appropriate Federal Role in Urban Transportation Planning. The comments clearly indicated the preference for fewer federal requirements and greater flexibility. Further indication of these views resulted from the Airlie House Conference on Urban Transportation Planning in the 1980s (Transportation Research Board, 1982b).

Based on the comments, the joint urban transportation planning regulations were rewritten to remove items that were not actually required. The changes in the regulations responded to the call for reducing the role of the federal government in urban transportation planning. The revised regulations, issued on June 30, 1983, contained new statutory requirements and retained the requirements for a transportation plan, a transportation improvement program (TIP) including an annual element (or biennial element), and a unified planning work program (UPWP), the latter only for areas of 200,000 or more in population. The planning process was to be self-certified by the states and MPOs as to its conformance with all requirements when submitting the TIP (U.S. DOT, 1983c).

The regulations drew a distinction between federal requirements and good planning practice. They stated the product or end that was required but left the details of the process to the state and local agencies. So the regulations no longer contained the elements of the process nor factors to consider in conducting the process (U.S. DOT, 1983c).

The urban transportation planning process was still the mutual responsibility of the MPO, state, and public transit operators. But, the nature of the MPO was to be the determination of Governor and local governments without any federal prescription. Governors were also given the option of administering the UMTA's planning funds for urban areas with populations under 200,000.

The revised regulations marked a major shift in the evolution of urban transportation planning. Up to that time, the response to new issues and problems was to create additional federal requirements. These regulations changed the focus of responsibility and control to the state and local governments. The federal government remained committed to urban planning by requiring that projects be based on a 3C planning process and by continuing to provide funding for planning activities. But it would no longer specify how the process was to be performed.

11
PRIVATE SECTOR PARTICIPATION

As the decade of the 1980s progressed there was a growing awareness that the public sector did not have the resources to continue providing all of the programs to which it had become committed. This was particularly true at the federal level of government. Moreover, by continuing these programs, governmental bodies were preempting areas that could be better served by the private sector. Governments and public agencies began to seek opportunities for greater participation of the private sector in the provision and financing of urban transportation facilities and services. In addition, the federal government sought to foster increased competition in the provision of transportation services as a means to increase efficiency and reduce costs. Changes in the transportation system were intended to be the outcomes of competition in the marketplace rather than of public regulation. This necessitated eliminating practices whereby unsubsidized private transportation service providers competed on an unequal basis with subsidized public agencies (Weiner, 1984).

Paratransit Policy

The range of public transportation services options known as "paratransit" was brought to national attention in a report by the Urban Institute (Kirby, et al., 1975). Paratransit-type services had already been receiving growing interest (Highway Research Board, 1971a; 1973b; Transportation Research Board, 1974a, 1974b; Rosenbloom, 1975; Scott, 1975). Paratransit was seen as a supplement to conventional transit that would serve special population groups and markets that were otherwise poorly served. It was also seen as an alternative, in certain circumstances, to conventional transit. It fit well into the tenor of the times, which sought low-cost alternatives to the automobile that could capture a larger share of the travel market. Paratransit could serve low density, dispersed travel patterns and thereby compete with the automobile.

The UMTA struggled for many years to develop a policy position on paratransit. The transit industry expressed concern about paratransit alternatives to conventional transit. Paratransit supporters saw it as the key option to compete against the automobile in low-density markets. It was the same debate that surfaced at the Woods Hole Conference on Future Directions of Urban Public Transportation (Transportation Research Board, 1984a).

Finally, in October 1982, the UMTA published the Paratransit Policy. Paratransit was portrayed as a supplement to conventional transit services that could increase transportation capacity at low cost. It could provide service in markets that were not viable for mass transit. Paratransit could also serve specialized markets (e.g., elderly and handicapped) and be an alternative to the private automobile. Its potential in rural areas was emphasized as well (U.S. DOT, 1982a).

The Paratransit Policy encouraged local areas to give full consideration to paratransit options. It supported the use of paratransit provided by private operators, particularly where they were not subsidized. The policy fostered reducing regulatory barriers to private operators, timely consultation with the private sector, matching services to travel needs, and integration of paratransit and conventional transit services (U.S. DOT, 1982a).

It was stated that UMTA funds were available for planning, equipment purchase, facility acquisition, capital, administrative, and research expenses. The UMTA preferred unsubsidized, privately provided paratransit, but would provide financial support where justified (U.S. DOT, 1982a).

Conferences on Goods Transportation in Urban Areas

The movement of goods in urban areas continued to be an important issue for planners, researchers, and decision makers after the Conference on Urban Commodity Flow in December 1970 had concluded that goods movement needed more emphasis in the urban transportation planning process. Considerable progress was made in the ensuing years in gaining a better understanding of goods movement issues and problems, and in development of courses of action to lead to their resolution.

To facilitate an exchange of experiences and ideas among those concerned about urban goods movement, a series of conferences sponsored by the Engineering Foundation was held under the title of Goods Transportation in Urban Areas: in August 1973 at South Berwick, Maine (Fisher, 1974); in September 1975 at Santa Barbara, California (Fisher, 1976); in December 1977 at Sea Island, Georgia (Fisher, 1978); and, in June 1981 at Easton, Maryland (Fisher and Meyburg, 1982).

The conferences highlighted the progress that had been made in identifying problems and analysis techniques, and discussed changes in institutional arrangements, regulations, and physical facilities to improve the movement of goods.

Yet, even after all of this work, most urban transportation planning processes gave little attention to the movement of goods. There still was no generally accepted methodology for urban goods movement planning; no urban areas had collected the necessary data to analyze commodity (as opposed to vehicle) flows; and a consensus had not been reached on the data items to collect. Attempts at system-level goods movement models and demand forecasting techniques had not been successful (Hedges, 1985).

The fourth conference on goods transportation occurred at a time when the pace of deregulation was increasing. In this deregulated environment, barriers to entry were being removed, limitations on rates and rate structures reduced, and the role of the public sector lessened. The emphasis shifted to transportation system-management approaches that sought to make more efficient use of existing facilities and equipment. These strategies had short implementation periods, addressed specific site problems, could be carried out in an incremental manner, and did not require extensive institutional coordination. Such approaches were appropriate for the deregulated environment that was emerging in which there was only limited interaction between the public and private sectors.

There remained after these conferences the need for a better understanding of the issues, more complete measurement of the phenemona, more thorough documentation of the accomplishments, and wider dissemination of the information. The creation of effective cooperation among those concerned about the goods movement problem, particularly the public and private sectors, was still being called for to improve the productivity of goods movement in urban areas (Fisher and Meyburg, 1982).

Revised Major Transit Capital Investment Policy

By the early 1980s there had been a huge upsurge of interest in building new urban rail transit systems and extensions to existing ones. Beginning in 1972 new urban rail systems had begun revenue service in San Francisco, Washington, D.C., Atlanta, Baltimore, San Diego, Miami, and Buffalo. Construction was underway for new systems in Portland, Oregon, Detroit, Sacramento, and San Jose. A total of 32 urban areas were conducting studies for major new transit investments in 46 corridors. It was estimated that if all of those projects were carried out, the cost to the federal government would have been at least $19 billion (U.S. DOT, 1984a).

The federal funds for rail projects came, for the most part, from the Section 3 Discretionary Grant program. This program was funded by the revenue from one cent of the five-cent increase in the user charge on motor fuels that was included in the Surface Transportation Assistance Act of 1982, and amounted to $1.1 billion annually. The UMTA, however, was giving priority to projects for rehabilitation of existing rail and bus systems. Only $400 million annually was targeted for use on new urban rail projects. The resulting gap between the demand for federal funds for major transit projects and those available was, therefore, very large.

In an attempt to manage the demand for federal funds, the UMTA issued a revised Urban Mass Transportation Major Capital Investment Policy on May 18, 1984 (U.S. DOT, 1984b). It was a further refinement of the evaluation process for major transit projects that had been evolving over a number of years. Under the policy, the UMTA would use the results of local planning studies to calculate the cost-effectiveness and local financial support for each project. These criteria would be used to rate the projects. The UMTA would fund only those projects that ranked high on both criteria to the extent that they did not exceed the available funds. The lower ranked projects were still eligible for funding if additional money became available.

The project development process involved a number of stages after which the UMTA would make a decision on whether to proceed to the next stage (See Fig. 11.1). The most critical decision occurred after the alternatives analysis and draft environmental impact statement (AA/DEIS) was completed. During this stage, the cost-effectiveness of new fixed guideway projects was compared to a base system called the "transportation system management" alternative. This TSM alternative consisted of an upgraded bus system plus other actions that would improve mobility with a minimal capital investment, such as parking management techniques, carpool and vanpool programs, traffic engineering improvements, and paratransit services. Often the marginal improvement in mobility of a fixed guideway proposal over the TSM was found to be not worth the cost to construct and operate it.

Projects were rated on cost-effectiveness and local fiscal effort after the AA/DEIS was completed. Local fiscal effort consisted of the level of funding from state, local, and private sources. In addition the projects had to meet several threshold criteria. First, the fixed guideway project had to generate more patronage than the TSM alternative. Second, the cost per additional rider of the fixed guideway project could not exceed a preset value that the UMTA was to determine. Third, the project had to meet all statutory and regulatory requirements.

The pressure for federal funds for new urban rail projects was so great, however, that the matter was often settled politically. Starting in fiscal year 1981, the Congress began to earmark Section 3 Discretionary Grant funds for specific projects, thereby preempting the UMTA from making the selection. The UMTA continued to rate the projects and make the information available to Congressional committees.

Private Participation in the Transit Program

The Reagan Administration was committed to a greater private sector role in addressing the needs of communities. They believed that governments at all

FIGURE 11.1. UMTA Project development process

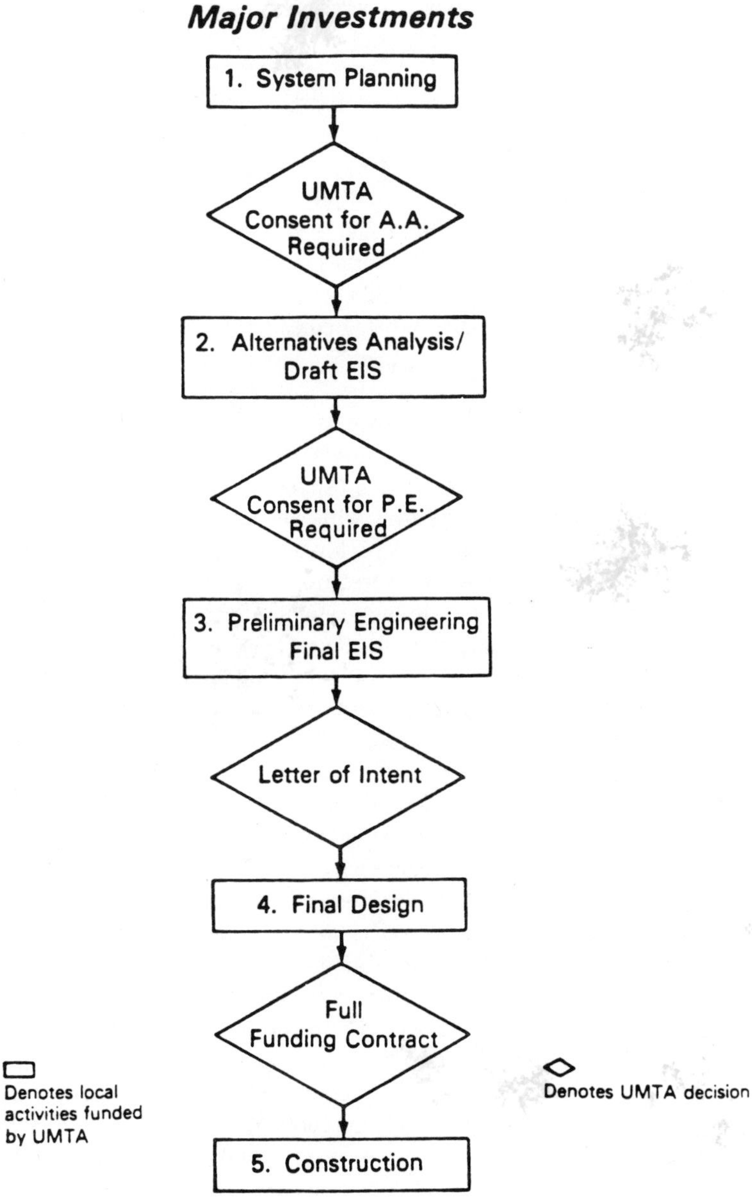

Major Investments

```
                    ┌─────────────────────┐
                    │  1. System Planning │
                    └─────────────────────┘
                              │
                              ▼
                         ◇─────────◇
                        UMTA
                   Consent for A.A.
                       Required
                         ◇─────────◇
                              │
                              ▼
                    ┌─────────────────────┐
                    │ 2. Alternatives     │
                    │    Analysis/        │
                    │    Draft EIS        │
                    └─────────────────────┘
                              │
                              ▼
                         ◇─────────◇
                        UMTA
                   Consent for P.E.
                       Required
                         ◇─────────◇
                              │
                              ▼
                    ┌─────────────────────┐
                    │ 3. Preliminary      │
                    │    Engineering      │
                    │    Final EIS        │
                    └─────────────────────┘
                              │
                              ▼
                         ◇─────────◇
                       Letter of Intent
                         ◇─────────◇
                              │
                              ▼
                    ┌─────────────────────┐
                    │  4. Final Design    │
                    └─────────────────────┘
                              │
                              ▼
                         ◇─────────◇
                           Full
                      Funding Contract
                         ◇─────────◇
                              │
                              ▼
                    ┌─────────────────────┐
                    │  5. Construction    │
                    └─────────────────────┘
```

▭
Denotes local
activities funded
by UMTA

◇
Denotes UMTA decision

levels should not provide services that the private sector was willing and able to provide, and that there would be increased efficiencies in an operating environment in which there was competition. Consequently, the Department of Transportation sought to remove barriers to greater involvement of the private sector in the provision of urban transportation services and in the financing of these services.

The instances of private provision of urban public transportation services and in public/private cooperative ventures had been increasing slowly. Transit agencies were having difficulty thinking in terms of private involvement in what they viewed as their business. Private transportation operators had voiced concerns that, in spite of statutory requirements, they were not being fully or fairly considered for the provision of public transportation service. But large operating deficits were creating pressure to find cheaper means to provide service, and private providers were increasingly being considered. Some transit agencies were beginning to contract out services that they found too expensive to provide themselves.

To promote increased involvement of the private sector in the provision of public transportation services, the UMTA issued a Policy on Private Participation in the Urban Mass Transportation Program (U.S. DOT, 1984c). It provided guidance for achieving compliance with several sections of the Urban Mass Transportation Act. Section 3(e) prohibited unfair competition with private providers by publicly subsidized operators. Section 8(e) required maximum participation of the private sector in the planning of public transportation services. Section 9(f), which was added by the Surface Transportation Assistance Act of 1982, established procedures for involving the private sector in the development of Transportation Improvement Program as a condition for federal funding.

The Policy on Private Participation in the Urban Mass Transportation Program called for early involvement of private providers in the development of new transit services and for their maximum feasible participation in providing those services. The policy identified the principal factors that the UMTA would consider in determining whether recipients complied with the statutes. It indicated that private transportation providers must be consulted in the development of plans for new and restructured services. Moreover, private carriers must be considered where new or restructured public transportation services were to be provided. A true comparison of costs was to be used when comparing publicly provided service with private providers. An independent local dispute resolution mechanism was to be established to assure fairness in administering the policy.

This policy represented a major departure from past federal policy toward public transportation operators. Where public operators had had a virtual monopoly on federal funds for transit facilities, equipment, and service, now they needed to consider private sector operators as competitors for providing those services.

Charter Bus Regulations

The Urban Mass Transportation Act of 1964 defined mass transportation to specifically exclude charter services. Federal assistance for mass transportation was, therefore, not to be used to provide such services. The federal government had thereby declared at the outset of the transit program that it confined its role to assisting only regular mass transit services. The Comptroller General ruled, however, in a 1966 case that buses purchased with federal funds could provide charter service if the service was incidental and did not interfere with the provision of regular transit services for which the buses were purchased.

As public transit agencies engaged in charter bus operations, there was a concern, generally raised by private bus operators, that public agencies were competing unfairly. The argument was that public agencies were using federal subsidies to allow them to underprice their services and thereby foreclose private operators from charter service markets. The Federal Aid Highway Act of 1973 sought to clarify the charter bus prohibition. It required all recipients of federal transit funds or highway funds to enter into an agreement with the Secretary of Transportation that they would not operate any charter service outside of their mass transportation service area in competition with private operators (U.S. DOT, 1982b).

The Housing and Community Development Act of 1974 gave the Secretary of Transportation the flexibility to tailor solutions to this problem to the individual situation. The agreements negotiated with recipients were to provide fair and equitable arrangements to assure that publicly and privately owned operators for public bodies did not foreclose private operators from the intercity charter bus industry where such operators were willing and able to provide such service. The National Mass Transportation Assistance Act of 1974 extended these charter bus provisions to federal financial assistance for operating expenses, which was a new category of federal assistance established by that act (U.S. DOT, 1982b).

Regulations to implement these charter bus provisions were published in April 1976 (U.S. DOT, 1976d). Under the regulations, a public transit operator could provide intercity or intracity charter bus service if it was incidental to the provision of mass transportation service. A service was considered incidental if it did not: (a) occur during peak hours, (b) require a trip more than 50 miles beyond the recipient's service area, or (c) require a particular for more than six hours. If a public operator provided intercity charter service, the charter revenues had to cover its total costs and the rates charged could not foreclose competition from private operators. Some 79 separate costs had to be accounted for in the public operator's certification.

Both public and private operators found the regulation unsatisfactory. Public operators supported easing the restrictions on their provision of charter bus service as a means to provide supplemental revenue and improve their financial condition. Private operators preferred tightening the restrictions and strengthening enforcement, which they felt was inadequate. Moreover it was clear that the recordkeeping and certification requirements on grant recipients was unnecessarily burdensome.

Finding a balance between the views of public and private operators was extremely difficult, and the UMTA struggled with the problem for a number of years. Shortly after issuing the regulation in 1976, the UMTA published an Advanced Notice of Proposed Rulemaking (ANPRM) requesting views on several issues and suggestions on how to make the regulation more effective. A public hearing was held in January 1977 to solicit additional comments. Afterward the UMTA issued two additional ANPRMs in an attempt to obtain the views of interested parties on a number of issues and possible options for modifying the regulation (U.S. DOT, 1981c, 1982b).

Finally, in March 1986 the UMTA published a revised regulation in the form of a NPRM (U.S. DOT, 1986). It would prohibit any UMTA recipient from providing charter bus service or using UMTA assistance if there was a private charter bus operator that was willing and able to provide the service. Only in the absence of willing and able operators or their lack of vehicles accessible to the handicapped could a public operator provide charter service. The determination of willing and able operators was to be made annually at a public hearing.

12
CONCLUSION

Urban transportation planning evolved from highway and transit planning activities in the 1930s and 1940s. These efforts were primarily intended to improve the design and operation of individual transportation facilities. The focus was on upgrading and expanding facilities.

Early urban transportation planning studies were primarily systems-oriented with a twenty-year time horizon and region-wide in scope. This was largely the result of legislation for the National System of Interstate and Defense Highways, which required that these major highways be designed for traffic projected twenty years into the future. As a result, the focus of the planning process through the decade of the 1960s was on this long-range time horizon and broad regional scale. Gradually, starting in the early 1970s, planning processes turned their attention to shorter-term time horizons and the corridor-level scale. This came about as the result of a realization that long-range planning had been dominated by concern for major regional highway and transit facilities with only minor attention being paid to lesser facilities with the opportunity to improve the efficiency of the existing system. This shift was reinforced by the increasing difficulties and cost in constructing new facilities, growing environmental concerns, and the Arab oil embargo.

Early efforts with programs such as TOPICS and express bus priorities eventually broadened into the strategy of transportation system management. TSM encompassed a whole range of techniques to increase the utilization and productivity of existing vehicles and facilities. It shifted the emphasis from facility expansion to provision of transportation service. The federal government took the lead in pressing for changes that would produce greater attention to TSM. At first there was considerable resistance. Neither institutions nor techniques were able immediately to address TSM options. A period of learning and adaptation was necessary to redirect planning processes so that they could perform this new

95

type of planning. As the 1980s dawned, urban transportation planning had become primarily short-term oriented in most urbanized areas.

Through this evolutionary development, the urban transportation planning process was called upon to address a continuous stream of new issues and concerns, methodological developments, advances in technology, and changing attitudes. Usually it was the requirements from the federal government to which the planning process was responding.

Major new issues began affecting urban transportation planning in the latter half of the 1960s and on through the 1970s. The list of issues included safety, citizen involvement, preservation of parkland and natural areas, equal opportunity for disadvantaged persons, environmental concerns (particularly air quality), transportation for the elderly and handicapped, energy conservation, and revitalization of urban centers. Most recently these have been joined by concerns for deterioration of the highway and transit infrastructure. By 1980 the federal requirements to address all of these matters had become extensive, complex, and sometimes conflicting.

During this same period there were advocates for various transportation options as solutions to this vast array of problems and concerns. They ranged over the gamut from new highways, express buses, rail transit systems, pricing, automated guideway transit, paratransit, brokerage, and dual-mode transit. It was difficult at times to determine whether these options were advanced as the answer to all of these problems or for just some of them. Transportation system management was an attempt to integrate the short-term, low capital options into reinforcing strategies to accomplish one or more objectives. Alternatives analysis was designed to evaluate tradeoffs among various major investments options as well as transportation system management techniques.

Transportation planning techniques also evolved during this time. Procedures for specific purposes were integrated into an urban travel forecasting process in the early urban transportation studies in the 1950s. Through the 1960s improvements in planning techniques were made primarily by practitioners, and these new approaches were integrated into practice fairly easily. The FHWA and UMTA carried out extensive activities to develop and disseminate analytical techniques and computer programs for use by state and local governments. The Urban Transportation Planning System (UTPS) became the standard computer battery for urban transportation analysis by the mid 1970s.

During the 1970s new techniques were developed for the most part by the research community, largely in universities. The disaggregate approaches differed from the aggregate approaches being used in practice. Communication between researchers and practitioners was fitful. While researchers were developing more appropriate ways of analyzing this complex array of issues and options, practitioners were still wedded to the older techniques. The gap between research and practice still needs to be closed.

The 1980s bring a new challenge to urban transportation planning, the decentralization of authority and responsibility. The national mood has shifted and centralized approaches are no longer considered to be the appropriate means for dealing with national problems. The federal government is reducing its involvement and leaving the states and local governments more flexibility to respond in whatever manner they choose. The federal statutes remain in force but additional federal guidance or elaboration is being reduced and eliminated.

It is unclear what changes will occur in urban transportation planning as a result of the reduction in federal regulation and prescription. There will be expanded opportunities to fashion planning procedures and institutions to local problems and needs. More time and effort can be used to produce the information for local decisions rather than to meet federal requirements. Urban areas experiencing growth in population and employment, for example, can focus on long-range development plans to expand their transportation systems. Other urban areas that are stable or declining can deal with redevelopment issues and infrastructure rehabilitation. There will be more flexibility in the elements of the planning process and in the division of responsibilities to perform them.

On the other hand, planning will have to be more responsive to the needs of local decision makers and citizens, and adjusted to the realities of long-term budget constraints in many urban areas. Procedures and institutional arrangements will have to be realigned to address local issues and needs. This may be difficult for urban transportation planning processes that have been attuned to federal requirements.

Many of the issues that have been debated over the last decade are likely to be revisited. One issue is the appropriate balance between long-range and short-term planning. A second is the level of effort devoted to system expansion, infrastructure rehabilitation, system management, and possibly even system retrenchment (e.g., removal of certain facilities or routes) to match declining population, travel demand, and financial resources. The issues of changing institutional arrangements and locus of decision making are likely to be raised in a number of urban areas.

Some urban areas will struggle with using transportation to foster economic development while still providing mobility. The use of innovative financing techniques such as joint development and increased participation by the private sector will probably increase to offset shortfalls in public sector funds. The matters of environmental quality, transportation for special groups, and energy conservation will likely be valued differently across the spectrum of urban areas and affect planning processes in these areas in different ways.

The level of detail and complexity of planning procedures will need to be reassessed. Smaller urban areas will likely opt for a simpler planning process that is commensurate with their fewer problems and less complex planning context. The larger areas will face many more choices in terms of problems to address, options to evaluate, organizational arrangements, and procedures to use. Transportation analysis may become better integrated with land-use planning at the project-level scale.

The planning community will be challenged to further adapt so that procedures and techniques are tailored to local requirements. Many new approaches were developed during the decade of the 1970s. New transportation options, travel analysis methods, and institutional structures were researched and applied in at least a limited fashion. The microcomputer holds the promise of providing analytical capability to many more agencies at lower cost with faster response time. All of these are now available to planners trying to reshape planning processes to the changing needs. The results should be evident within the next few years.

APPENDIX

Chronology of Significant Events

1916 – Federal Aid Road Act: created Bureau of Public Roads, beginning of federal aid highway program
1921 – Federal Highway Act: required state highway departments, established federal-aid highway system, contract authority, state matching

Early Highway Planning

1934 – Federal Aid Highway Act: 1.5 percent HP&R Program (permissive), statewide highway planning surveys begun
1937 – *Toll Roads and Free Roads* report
1941 – Interregional Highways report

Beginnings of Urban Transportation Planning

1944 – First Home Interview Manual published
Federal Aid Highway Act: established federal aid Secondary and Urban Extensions programs, directed designation of 40,000 mile national system of Interstate highways, but provided no funding
1945 – Chicago Transit Authority (CTA) created
1947 – Housing Act: created Housing and Home Finance Agency (HHFA)
MTA created in Boston
1948 – San Juan, Puerto Rico transportation study—trip generation by land use type
1950 – TRB Compendium of O-D practices published
1953 – Federal Aid Highway Act: first funding for Interstate system
1953 – Detroit Metropolitan Area Traffic Study (DMATS) started—used tabulating machines
1954 – Housing Act: established 701 Comprehensive Urban Planning Program
1955 – A.M. Voorhees' Gravity Model
Chicago Area Transportation Study (CATS) started—prototype for future urban transportation studies
Washington Metropolitan Area Traffic Study (WMATS) started

1956 – Federal Aid Highway Act: created funding for National System of Interstate and Defense Highways

Highway Revenue Act: established Highway Trust Fund, 90 percent federal share

San Francisco Rapid Transit Commission recommends 123 mile system

Highway Traffic Estimation published—highlights Fratar technique

1957 – Traffic assignment algorithms

Baltimore Transportation Study started

1958 – Pittsburgh Area Transportation Study (PATS) started

Hartford Area Traffic Study started

National Committee on Urban Transportation, *Better Transportation For Your City* published

Sagamore Conference on Highways and Urban Development—regionwide comprehensive planning

1959 – Penn-Jersey (Philadelphia) Transportation Study started

1961 – Housing Act: created program of transit loans and demonstration grants, allowed 701 funds for urban transportation studies

Urban Transportation Planning Comes of Age

1962 – Joint Report on Urban Mass Transportation

President Kennedy's Transportation Message

Federal Aid Highway Act: mandated 3C urban transportation planning process, 1.5 percent required for HP&R purposes, 0.5 percent optional

Hershey Conference on Freeways in the Urban Setting

Bay Area rapid transit system bond issue passed

1963 – IM 50-2-63 Guidelines for 3C planning process—defined 3C process including 10 elements

1964 – Urban Mass Transportation Act: created transit capital grants (66.67 percent federal share), R&D program

Improved Intergovernmental Coordination

1965 – Housing and Urban Development Act: created HUD, 701 grants for comprehensive planning to COGs and Regional Planning Councils

Williamsburg Conference on Highways and Urban Development—social and community values

1966 – Department of Transportation Act: created DOT

Amendments to the Urban Mass Transportation Act: created transit technical studies program, management training grants, New Systems study

Demonstration Cities and Metropolitan Development Act: created 204 Review area wide process for federal aid projects, Model Cities program

1967 – PPM 50-9: consolidated previous guidance on urban transportation planning

Dartmouth Conference on Urban Development Models

1968 – Federal Aid Highway Act: created TOPICS, prohibited takings of parks, wetlands or wildlife refuge, required public hearings

Reorganization Plan No. 2: established Urban Mass Transportation Administration (UMT) in DOT

Intergovernmental Cooperation Act: required coordination of federal programs with local governments

IM 50-4-68: Operations Plans for "Continuing" Urban Transportation Planning—five elements: surveillance, reappraisal, service, procedural development and annual report

Tomorrow's Transportation: New Systems for the Urban Future

Environment and Two-Hearing Process

1969 – National Environmental Policy Act (NEPA): created EIS process, established CEQ, required systematic, interdisciplinary approach to planning and decision making

A-95 Project Notification and Review Process: required area-wide planning agencies to comment on federally-aided projects

PPM 20-8, Two Hearing Process: required full consideration of social, economic, and environmental impacts

Environmental Quality Improvement Act: established Office of Environmental Quality

Beginnings of Multimodal Urban Transportation Planning

1970 – Urban Mass Transportation Assistance Act: established long term commitment of transit funds, $10 billion over 12 years, Elderly and Handicapped requirements

Clean Air Act Amendments: created EPA, emission standards specified, required national ambient air quality standards be established, SIPs and TCPs, focus on traffic management

Federal Aid Highway Act: Federal Aid Urban system (FAUS), 70 percent federal share for non-Interstate projects, local selection of routes, allowed highway funds for bus projects, required guidelines on economic, social and environmental impacts, required guidelines for highway project consistency with SIPs

Mt. Pocono Conference on Urban Transportation Planning

Boston Transportation Planning Review

1971 – IM 50-3-71: established annual certification of 3C process

1972 – PPM 90-4: Process Guidelines for Highway Projects

Williamsburg Conference on Urban Travel Forecasting

UMTA's External Operating Manual: described planning requirements for transit projects

1973 – Federal Aid Highway Act: allowed FAUS and Interstate funds to be transferred to transit projects

Rehabilitation Act: Section 504 access for elderly and handicapped persons

CEQ guidelines on preparation of EISs

1974 – National Mass Transportation Assistance Act: authorized federal transit operating assistance, federal share 80 percent for capital and 50 percent for operating projects, same planning regs as highways, 0.5 fare for E+H, rural program

Transition to Short-Term Planning

1973 – OPEC Oil Embargo

1974 – Emergency Highway Energy Conservation Act: 55 mph speed limit

1975 – Energy Policy and Conservation Act: established CAFE standards

Joint FHWA/UMTA planning regulations: required MPOs, Prospectus, UPWP, TIP & Annual Element (AE), TSM measures

Office of Technology Assessment's Report on *Automated Guideway Transit*—SLT, GRT, PRT

1976 – Policy on Major Urban Mass Transportation Investments: established criteria of multimodal, region-wide planning, incremental implementation, TSM measures, cost-effectiveness

Federal Aid Highway Act: allowed Interstate transfers to other highways and busways, established 3R program

Section 504 Regulations: special efforts, suggested 5 percent of funds

1977 – Clean Air Act Amendments: extended deadlines, required "conformance" and "sanctions"

Department of Energy Organization Act: created DOE

National Urban Development and New Communities Development Act: required National Urban Policy Report rather than report on growth

Urban Economic Development

1978 – National Urban Policy Report: revitalization of central cities and older suburbs

Policy Toward Rail Transit: required high density corridors, local supporting policies

National Energy Act: energy conservation goal, promote carpools and vanpools

Surface Transportation Assistance Act: Interstate completion deadline of 1990: projects under contract by Sept. 1986, I-substitutions by Sept. 1983, created bridge R&R program, transit Section 5 program expanded to four tiers, rural program, same planning requirement for highways and transit, "Buy America" requirement

Council on Environmental Quality's Regulations: "scoping" and "tiering"

Transportation and Air Quality guidelines: integrated air quality planning into the 3C planning process

Aspen Conference on Future Urban Transportation: automobile will continue to be dominant mode

1979 – Urban Initiatives program guidelines: joint development, leveraging federal investments, stimulate economic development

Final Section 504 Regulations on Accessibility for the Handicapped: full access in 3 years, 50 percent of buses

1980 – Joint FHWA/UMTA Environmental regulations: single set of environmental procedures of highway and transit projects, single EIS/AA document

Decentralization of Decision Making

1981 – Air Quality Conformance and Priority Procedures

President Reagan's Memorandum on Regulations: postponed regulations for 60 days

Executive Order 12291: procedures for evaluating regulations, benefits must exceed costs

Interim Section 504 regulations: certify special efforts were being made

1982 – Airlie House Conference on Urban Transportation Planning in the 1980s: need for greater flexibility and reduced requirements

Executive Order 12372 Intergovernmental Review of Federal Programs: replaced A-95, states establish own review process, federal government must "accommodate" or "explain," "single point of contact"

Woods Hole Conference on Future Directions of Urban Public Transportation: split between conventional transit and paratransit advocates

Easton Conference on Travel Analysis Methods for the 1980s: gap between research and practice

Surface Transportation Assistance Act of 1982: 5 cent increase in gas tax; revenue from 4 cents to highways for Interstate completion and expanded highway and bridge rehabilitation; revenue from other 1 cent into Mass Transit Account of Highway Trust Fund for Discretionary Grants only for capital needs (75 percent federal share), new Section 9 Formula Grant program for capital and operating projects (cap on operating assistance)

Paratransit Policy: encouraged paratransit as supplement or substitute for conventional transit

Revised Urban Transportation Planning Regulations: removed all items not actually required, increased state and local flexibility

1983 – Advent of Microcomputers

Section 504 Regulations (NPRM): DOT-wide, detailed criteria

Private Sector Participation

1984 – Urban Mass Transportation Major Capital Investment Policy (Notice): specified cost-effectiveness measures

Policy on User-side Subsidies: eligible for federal funds

Policy on Private Enterprise Participation in the Urban Mass Transportation Program

1986 – Charter Bus Regulations (NPRM): would prohibit charter bus services by public transit operators unless no one willing and able

LIST OF ABBREVIATIONS

AASHO	American Association of State Highway Officials
AGT	Automated Guideway Transit
ANPRM	Advanced Notice of Proposed Rulemaking
BOB	Bureau of the Budget
BPR	Bureau of Public Roads
3C	Continuing, Comprehensive, and Cooperative
CAFE	Corporate Average Fuel Economy
CATS	Chicago Area Transportation Study
CEQ	Council on Environmental Quality
COG	Council of Governments
DMATS	Detroit Metropolitan Area Traffic Study
DPM	Downtown People Mover
DOE	Department of Energy
DOT	Department of Transportation
EIS	Environmental Impact Statement
EPA	Environmental Protection Agency
FAUS	Federal Aid Urban System
FHWA	Federal Highway Administration
FONSI	Finding of No Significant Impact
FY	Fiscal Year
GRT	Group Rapid Transit
HEW	Department of Health, Education, and Welfare
HHFA	Housing and Home Finance Agency
HHS	Department of Health and Human Services
HP&R	Highway Planning and Research
HRB	Highway Research Board
ICE	Interstate Cost Estimate
HUD	Department of Housing and Urban Development
IM	Instructional Memorandum
IPG	Intermodal Planning Group
LRV	Light Rail Vehicle
MPO	Metropolitan Planning Organization
NEPA	National Environmental Policy Act of 1969

NPRM	Notice of Proposed Rulemaking
OMB	Office of Management and Budget
OTA	Office of Technology Assessment
PATS	Pittsburgh Area Transportation Study
PLANPAC	Planning Package (of computer programs)
PPM	Policy and Procedure Memorandum
PRT	Personal Rapid Transit
3R	Resurfacing, Restoration, and Rehabilitation
4R	Resurfacing, Restoration, Rehabilitation, and Reconstruction
SIP	State Implementation Plan
SLRV	Standard Light Rail Vehicle
SLT	Shuttle Loop Transit
SMD	Service and Methods Demonstration
SMSA	Standard Metropolitan Statistical Area
TCP	Transportation Control Plan
TIP	Transportation Improvement Program
TRB	Transportation Research Board
TSM	Transportation System Management
UMTA	Urban Mass Transportation Administration
UPWP	Unified Planning Work Program
UTPS	Urban Transportation Planning System

REFERENCES

Advisory Commission on Intergovernmental Relations. 1974. "Toward more balanced transportation: New intergovernmental proposals," Report A-49. U.S. Government Printing Office (hereafter U.S. GPO), Washington, D.C.

Allen, John. 1985. "Post-classical transportation studies," *Transportation Quarterly*, 39, No. 3 (July).

American Association of State Highway Officials. 1952. "A basis for estimating traffic diversion to new highway in urban areas," 38th Annual Meeting, Kansas City, Kansas (December).

American Planning Association. (June) 1979. Proceedings of the Aspen Conference on Future Urban Transportation. Chicago, IL: American Planning Assoc.

Bloch, Arnold J., Michael B. Gerard, and William H. Crowell. (December) 1982. *The Interstate Highway Trade-In Process* (2 vols.). Brooklyn, NY: Polytechnic Institute of New York.

Brand, Daniel and Marvin L. Manheim (eds.). 1973. "Urban travel demand forecasting," Special Report 143. Washington, D.C.: Highway Research Board.

Cabot Consulting Group. (May) 1982. *Transportation Energy Contingency Planning: Transit Fuel Supplies Under Decontrol*. Washington, D.C.: U.S. Department of Transportation (hereafter U.S. DOT).

Campbell, M. Earl. 1950. *Route Selection and Traffic Assignment*. Washington, D.C.: Highway Research Board.

Chappell, Charles W. Jr. and Mary T. Smith. 1971. "Review of urban goods movement studies, urban commodity flow," Special Report 120. Washington, D.C.: Highway Research Board.

Chicago Area Transportation Study (CATS) 1959–1962. *Study Findings* (vol. I, Dec. 1959); *Data Projections* (vol. II July 1960); *Transportation Plan* (vol. III, April 1962); Chicago, IL: Harrison Lith.

Cole, Leon Monroe (ed.). (May) 1968. "Tomorrow's transportation: New systems for the urban future," prepared by U.S. Department of Housing and Urban Development (hereafter U.S. HUD). Washington, D.C.: U. S. GPO.

Cooper, Norman L. and John O. Hidinger. 1980. *Integration of Air Quality and Transportation Planning, Transportation and the 1977 Clean Air Act Amendments*. New York: American Society of Civil Engineers.

Council on Environmental Quality. 1978. National Environmental Policy Act—Regulations, *Federal Register*, 43, No. 230 (November 29), pp. 55978–56007.

Creighton, Roger L. 1970. *Urban Transportation Planning*. Urbana, IL: Univ. Illinois Press.

Cron, Frederick, W. 1975. "Highway design for motor vehicles—An historical review, Part 2: The beginnings of traffic research." *Public Roads*, 38, no. 4 (March), pp. 163–74.

Detroit Metropolitan Area Traffic Study. July 1955/March 1956. Part I: *Data Summary and Interpretation*; Part II: *Future Traffic and a Long Range Expressway Plan*. Lansing, MI: Speaker-Hines and Thomas, State Printers.

Diamant, E.S., et al. 1976. *Light Rail Transit: State of the Art Review*. Springfield, IL: De Leuw, Cather & Co.

Domestic Council, Executive Office of the President. (May) 1976. *1976 Report on National Growth and Development—The Changing Issue for National Growth*, U.S. HUD. Washington, D.C.: U.S. GPO.

——. (February) 1972. *Report on National Growth—1972*. Washington, D.C.: U.S. GPO.

Fertal, Martin J., Edward Weiner, Arthur J. Balek, and Ali F. Sevin. (December) 1966. *Modal Split—Documentation of Nine Methods for Estimating Transit Usage*, U.S. Department of Commerce, Bureau of Public Roads. Washington, D.C.: U.S. GPO.

Fisher, Gordon P. (ed.). (June) 1978. *Goods Transportation in Urban Areas—Proceedings of the Engineering Foundation Conference, Sea Island, Georgia, December 4–9, 1977*. U.S. DOT.

——. (May) 1976. *Goods Transportation in Urban Areas—Proceedings of the Engineering Foundation Conference, Santa Barbara, California, September 7–12, 1975*. U.S. DOT.

——. (February) 1974. *Goods Transportation in Urban Areas—Proceedings of the Engineering Foundation Conference, Berwick Academy, South Berwick, Maine, August 5–10, 1973*. U.S. DOT.

Fisher, Gordon P. and Arnim H. Meyburg (eds.). (January) 1982. *Goods Transportation in Urban Areas—Proceedings of the Engineering Foundation Conference, Easton, Maryland, June 14–19, 1981*. U.S. DOT.

Gakenheimer, Ralph A. 1976. *Transportation Planning as Response to Controversy: The Boston Case*. Cambridge, MA: MIT Press.

Gakenheimer, Ralph and Michael Meyer. (November) 1977. *Transportation System Management: Its Origins, Local Response and Problems as a New Form of Planning*, Interim Report. Cambridge, MA: MIT.

Gortmaker, Linda (October) 1980. *Transportation and Urban Development*, U.S. Conference of Mayors. Washington, D.C.: U.S. GPO.

Harris, Britton (ed.). 1965. "Urban development models: New tools for planning," *J. Amer. Instit. Planners*, 31, No. 2 (May).

Hassell, John S. 1982. "How effective has urban transportation been?" in *Urban Transportation: Perspectives and Prospects*, edited by Herbert S. Levenson and Robert A. Weant. Westport, CT: Eno Foundation for Transportation.

Heanue, Kevin E. 1980. "Urban transportation planning—Are new directions needed for the 1980s?" Presented at the American Planning Association Conference, San Francisco, CA, April, 1980.

——. 1977. "Changing emphasis in urban transportation planning." Presented at the 56th Annual Meeting of the Transportation Board, Washington, D.C., January, 1977.

Hedges, Charles A. 1985. "Improving urban goods movement: The transportation management approach," in *Transportation Policy and Decisionmaking*, Vol. 3. The Netherlands: Martinus Nijhoff, pp. 113–133.

Hemmens, George C. 1968. *Urban Development Models,* Special Report 97. Washington, D.C.: Highway Research Board.

Hensher, David A. and Peter R. Stopher (eds.). 1979. *Behavioral Travel Modeling.* London: Croom Helm.

Herman, Frank V. (June) 1964. *Population Forecasting Methods.* Washington, D.C.: U.S. Department of Commerce, Bureau of Public Roads.

Hershey Conference. (June) 1962. Freeways in the Urban Setting. Sponsored by American Association of State Highway Officials, American Municipal Association, and National Association of County Officials. Washington, D.C.: Automotive Safety Foundation.

Highway Research Board. 1973a. *Organization for Continuing Urban Transportation Planning,* Special Report 139. Washington, D.C.: Highway Research Board.

——. 1973b. *Demand-Responsive Transportation Systems,* Special Report 136. Washington, D.C.: Highway Research Board.

——. 1971a. *Demand-Actuated Transportation Systems,* Special Report 124. Washington, D.C.: Highway Research Board.

——. 1971b. *Urban Commodity Flow,* Special Report 120. Washington, D.C.: Highway Research Board.

Highways and Urban Development. (December) 1965. Report on the Second National Conference, Williamsburg, Virginia, 1965, sponsored by American Association of State Highway Officials, National Association of Counties, and National League of Cities.

Holmes, E. H. 1962. "Highway planning in the United States" (unpublished, Madrid, Spain).

——. 1964. "Transit and federal highways." Presented at The Engineers' Club of St. Louis, U.S. Department of Commerce, April 23.

——. 1973. "The state-of-the-art in urban transportation planning, or how we got here." *Transportation,* I, no. 4 (March), pp. 379–401.

—— and J. T. Lynch. 1957. "Highway planning: Past, present, and future." *J. Highway Division* (Proceedings of the ASCE), 83, no. HW3 (July) 1298-1–1298-13.

Homburger, Wolfgang S. (ed.). 1967. *Urban Mass Transit Planning.* Berkeley: Univ. California Institute of Transportation and Traffic Engineering.

Humphrey, Thomas F. 1974. "Reappraising metropolitan transportation needs," *Transportation Engineering Journal, Proc. Amer. Soc. Civil Eng.* 100, No. TE2 (May).

Kirby, Ronald F., Kiran V. Bhatt, Michael A. Kemp, Robert G. McGillivray, and Martin Wohl. 1975. *Para-Transit: Neglected Options for Urban Mobility.* Washington, D.C.: The Urban Institute.

Kuehn, Thomas J. (August) 1976. *The Development of National Highway Policy.* Seattle: Univ. Washington.

Lee, R. B., W. Kudlick, J. C. Falcocchio, E.J. Cantilli, and A. Stefanivk. (February) 1978. *Review of Local Alternatives—Analyses Involving Automated Guideway Transit.* New York: Urbitran Associates.

Levinson, Herbert S., et al. 1973. *Bus Use of Highways: State of the Art,* National Cooperative Highway Research Program Report 143. Washington, D.C.: Highway Research Board.

Lieb, Robert C. (May) 1976. *Labor in the Transit Industry.* Boston: Northeastern Univ.

Mabee, Nancy and Barbara A. Zumwalt. (December) 1977. *Review of Downtown People Mover Proposals: Preliminary Market Implications for Downtown Application of*

Automated Guideway Transit. McLean, VA: Mitre Corporation.

Marple, Garland E. 1969. "Urban areas make transportation plans." Presented at the 1969 American Society of Civil Engineers Meeting of Transportation Engineering.

Meck, Joseph P. (August) 1965. *The Role of Economic Studies in Urban Transportation Planning.* Washington, D.C.: U.S. Department of Commerce, Bureau of Public Roads, U.S. GPO.

Metropolitan Transportation Commission (December) 1979a. *BART in the San Francisco Bay Area—Summary of the Final Report of the BART Impact Program.* Washington, D.C.: U.S. Department of Transportation.

———. (September) 1979b. *BART in the San Francisco Bay Area—The Final Report of the BART Impact Program.* Washington, D.C.: U.S. Department of Transportation.

Miller, David R. (ed.). 1972. *Urban Transportation Policy: New Perspectives.* Lexington, MA: Lexington Books.

Mitchell, Robert B. and Rapkin, Chester. 1954. *Urban Traffic: A Function of Land Use.* New York: Columbia Univ. Press.

National Committee on Urban Transportation. 1958. *Better Transportation for Your City: A Guide to the Factual Development of Urban Transportation Plans* (including 17 procedure manuals). Chicago, IL: Public Administration Service.

Paparella, Vincent F. 1982. *An Administrative History of the Development of the FHWA/UMTA Joint Urban Transportation Planning Regulations.* Washington, D.C.: U.S. DOT, Urban Mass Transportation Administration.

Parker, Elizabeth A. 1977. *Major Changes in the Urban and Rural Highway and Transit Programs.* Washington, D.C.: U.S. DOT.

Putman, Stephen H. 1979. *Urban Residential Location Models.* Boston, MA: Martinus Nijhoff.

Reagan, Ronald. 1981b. (January 29). "Postponement of pending regulations" (White House Memorandum).

———. 1981a. Federal Regulation, Executive Order 12291. *Federal Register,* 46, No. 33 (February 17), pp. 13193–98.

———. 1982. Intergovernmental Review of Federal Programs, Executive Order 12372. *Federal Register,* 47, No. 137 (July 16), pp. 30959–60.

Rice Center. (March 12) 1981. *Urban Initiatives Program Evaluation.* Houston, TX: Rice Center.

Rosenbloom, Sandra. 1975. *Paratransit,* Special Report 164. Washington, D.C.: Transportation Research Board.

Sagamore Conference on Highways and Urban Development. (October) 1958. *Guidelines for Action.* Conference sponsored by American Municipal Association, American Association of State Highway Officials, Highway Research Board, and Syracuse University.

Schmidt, Robert E. and M. Earl Campbell. 1956. *Highway Traffic Estimation.* Saugatuck, CT: Eno Foundation for Highway Traffic Control.

Schueftan, Oliver and Raymond H. Ellis. (February) 1981. *Federal, State and Local Responses to 1979 Fuel Shortages.* Washington, D.C.: Peat, Marwick, Mitchell & Co.

Scott, James A. 1975. "Paratransit" (Special Issue), *Transportation,* 4, No. 4 (December), Amsterdam, The Netherlands: Elsevier Scientific.

Silien Joseph S. and Jeffrey G. Mora. 1975. *North American Light Rail Vehicles, Light Rail Transit,* Special Report 161. Washington, D.C.: Transportation Research Board.

Silver, Jacob and Joseph R. Stowers. (July) 1964. *Population, Economic, and Land Use*

Studies in Urban Transportation Planning. Washington, D.C.: U.S. Department of Commerce, Bureau of Public Roads.

Smerk, George M. (ed.). 1968. *Readings in Urban Transportation.* Bloomington, IN: Indiana Univ. Press.

Spear, Bruce, et al. (December) 1981. *Service and Methods Demonstration Program, Annual Report.* Washington, D.C.: U.S. DOT, UMTA.

———. (August) 1979. *Service and Methods Demonstration Program, Annual Report.* Washington, D.C.: U.S. DOT, UMTA.

Stopher, Peter R., Arnim H. Meyburg, and Werner Brog. (eds.). 1981. *New Horizons in Travel-Behavior Research.* Lexington, MA: D.C. Heath.

Stopher, Peter R. and Arnim H. Meyburg (eds.). 1976. *Behavioral Travel-Demand Models.* Lexington, MA: D.C. Heath.

———. 1974. *Behavioral Modeling and Valuation of Travel Time,* Special Report 149. Washington, D.C.: Transportation Research Board.

Swerdloff, Carl N. and Joseph R. Stowers. 1966. *A Test of Some First Generation Residential Land Use Models,* Highway Research Record. No. 126. Washington, D.C.: Highway Research Board.

Transportation Research Board. 1985. *Light Rail Transit: System Design for Cost-Effectiveness,* State-of-the-Art Report 2. Washington, D.C.

———. 1984a. *Future Directions of Urban Public Transportation,* Special Report 200. Washington, D.C.

———. 1984b. *Travel Analysis Methods for the 1980s,* Special Report 201. Washington, D.C.

———. 1982a. *Light Rail Transit: Planning, Design and Implementation,* Special Report 195. Washington, D.C.

———. 1982b. *Urban Transportation Planning in the 1980s,* Special Report 196. Washington, D.C.

———. 1978. *Light Rail Transit: Planning and Technology,* Special Report 182. Washington, D.C.

———. 1977. *Urban Transportation Alternatives: Evolution of Federal Policy,* Special Report 177. Washington, D.C.

———. (February). 1975a. *A Review of Urban Mass Transportation Guidelines for Evaluation of Urban Transportation Alternatives,* A Report on the Conference on Evaluation of Urban Transportation Alternatives, Washington, D.C.

———. 1975b. *Light Rail Transit,* Special Report 161. Washington, D.C.

———. 1974a. *Demand-Responsive Transportation,* Special Report 147. Washington, D.C.

———. 1974b. *Demand-Responsive Transportation Systems and Services,* Special Report 154. Washington, D.C.

Transportation Systems Center. 1977. *Light Rail Transit: State of the Art Review.* Washington, D.C.: U.S. DOT.

U.S. Congress. 1975. The 1974 National Highway Needs Report, House Document No. 94-45, 94th Congress, 1st Session, U.S. Government Printing Office, Washington, D.C., February 10.

———. (August) 1972. Report to Congress on Section 109(h), Title 23, U.S. Code—Guidelines Relating to thee Economic, Social and Environmental Effects of Highway Projects. House Document No. 45, 92nd Congress, 2d Session. Washington, D.C.: U.S. GPO.

———. 1972a. Part 1 of the 1972 National Highway Needs Report, House Document No.

92-266, 92nd Congress, 2d Session, U.S. Government Printing Office, Washington, D.C., March 15.

———. 1972b. Part 2 of the 1972 National Highway Needs Report, House Document No. 92-266, Part II, 92nd Congress, 2d Session, U.S. Government Printing Office, Washington, D.C., April 10.

———. 1970. National Highway Needs Report With Supplement, Committee Print 91-28, 91st Congress, 2d Session, U.S. Government Printing Office, Washington, D.C., September.

———. 1968a, 1968. National Highway Needs Report, Committee Print 90-22, 90th Congress, 2d Session, U.S. Government Printing Office, Washington, D.C., February.

———. 1968b. Supplement to the 1968 National Highway Needs Report, Committee Print 90-22A, 90th Congress, 2d Session, U.S. Government Printing Office, Washington, D.C., July.

———. 1944. Interregional Highways, Message from the President of the United States Transmitting a Report of the National Interregional Highway Committee, House Document no. 379, 78th Congress, 2nd Session. Washington, D.C.: U.S. GPO.

———. 1939. Toll Roads and Free Roads, House Document no. 272, 76th Congress, 1st Session. Washington, D.C.: U.S. GPO.

U.S. Congress, Office of Technology Assessment. (June) 1975. *Automated Guideway Transit—An Assessment of PRT and Other New Systems*. Washington, D.C.: U.S. GPO.

U.S. Congress, Senate. 1962. Urban Transportation—Joint Report to the President by the Secretary of Commerce and the Housing and Home Finance Administration, Urban Mass Transportation—1962, 87th Congress, 2nd Session. Washington, D.C.: U.S. GPO., pp. 71-81.

U.S. Department of Commerce, Bureau of Public Roads. 1965a. *Highway Progress: Annual Report of the Bureau of Public Roads, Fiscal Year 1965*. Washington, D.C.: U.S. GPO.

———. (September) 1965b. *Traffic Assignment and Distribution for Small Urban Areas*. Washington, D.C.: U.S. GPO.

———. (June) 1964. *Traffic Assignment Manual*. Washington, D.C.: U.S. GPO.

———. (October) 1963a. *Calibrating and Testing a Gravity Model with a Small Computer*. Washington, D.C.: U.S. GPO.

———. (July) 1963b. *Calibrating and Testing a Gravity Model for Any Size Urban Area*. Washington, D.C.: U.S. GPO.

———. (March 27) 1963c. Instructional Memorandum 50-2-63, Urban Transportation Planning. Washington, D.C.: U.S. GPO.

———. (May) 1962. *Increasing the Traffic-Carrying Capability of Urban Arterial Streets: The Wisconsin Avenue Study*. Washington, D.C.: U.S. GPO.

———. (January) 1957. *The Administration of Federal Aid for Highways*. Washington, D.C.: U.S. GPO.

———. 1944. *Manual of Procedures for Home Interview Traffic Studies*. Washington, D.C.

U.S. Department of Energy. (November) 1978. *The National Energy Act—Information Kit*. Washington, D.C.

U.S. Department of Housing and Urban Development. (August) 1980. *The President's 1980 National Urban Policy Report*. Washington, D.C.: U.S. GPO.

U.S. Department of Housing and Urban Development. (March) 1978a. *A New Partner-*

ship to Conserve America's Communities—A National Urban Policy. Washington, D.C.: Urban and Regional Policy Group.

——. (December) 1978b. *The President's 1978 National Urban Policy Report*. Washington, D.C.: U.S. GPO.

U.S. Department of Transportation (Urban Mass Transportation Administration [UMTA]). 1986. Charter Bus Operations, *Federal Register*, 51, No. 44 (March 6), pp. 7892–7906.

——. (UMTA). (May 18) 1984a. "Stanley announces policy for new fixed guideway systems" (News Release), UMTA 16—84.

——. (UMTA). 1984b. Urban Mass Transportation Major Capital Investment Policy, *Federal Register*, 49, No. 98 (May 18), pp. 21284–91.

——. (UMTA). 1984c. Private Enterprise Participation in the Urban Mass Transportation Program, *Federal Register*, 49, No. 205 (October 22), pp. 41310–12.

——. 1983a. Intergovernmental Review of the Department of Transportation Programs and Activities, *Federal Register*, 48, No. 123 (June 24), pp. 29264–74.

——. (UMTA). (March) 1983b. AGT Socio-Economic Research Program Digest. Washington, D.C.

——. (Federal Highway Administration [FHWA] and UMTA). 1983c. Urban Transportation Planning, *Federal Register*, 48, No. 127 (June 30), pp. 30332–43.

——. (UMTA and FHWA). (September) 1983d. *Microcomputers in Transportation Software and Source Book*. Washington, D.C.: U.S. DOT.

——. (UMTA and FHWA). 1983e. *Microcomputers in Transportation, Selected Readings: Getting Started in Microcomputers* (Vol. 1); *Selecting a Single User System* (Vol. 2). Washington, D.C.: U.S. DOT.

——. (UMTA). 1982a. Paratransit Policy, *Federal Register*, 47, No. 201 (October 18), pp. 46410–11.

——. (UMTA). 1982b. Charter Bus Operations and School Bus Operations (ANPRM), *Federal Register*, 47, No. 197 (October 12), pp. 44795–804.

——. 1981a. Nondiscrimination on the Basis of Handicap, *Federal Register*, 46, No. 138 (July 20), pp. 37488–94.

——. (FHWA and UMTA). 1981b. Air Quality Conformity and Priority Procedures for Use in Federal-Aid Highway and Federally-Funded Transit Programs, *Federal Register*, 46, No. 16 (January 26), pp. 8426–32.

——. (UMTA). 1981c. Charter Bus Operations, *Federal Register*, 46, No. 12 (January 19), pp. 5394–407.

——. (FHWA). 1980a. *Federal Laws and Material Relating to the Federal Highway Administration*. Washington, D.C.: U.S. GPO.

——. (FHWA and UMTA). 1980b. Environmental Impact and Related Procedures, *Federal Register*, 45, No. 212 (October 30), pp. 71968–87.

——. 1980c. Energy Conservation by Recipients of Federal Financial Assistance, *Federal Register*, 45, No. 170 (August 29), pp. 58022–38.

——. (FHWA). 1979a. *America's Highways, 1776–1976, A History of the Federal-Aid Program*. Washington, D.C.: U.S. GPO.

——. (UMTA). 1979b. *Urban Mass Transportation Act of 1964, as amended through December 1978, and Related Laws*. Washington, D.C.: U.S. GPO.

——. (January) 1979c. *Energy Conservation in Transportation*. Washington, D.C.: U.S. DOT.

——. (August) 1979d. *The Surface Transportation Assistance Act of 1978.* Washington, D.C.: U.S. DOT.

——. (October 11) 1979e. "Improving the Urban Transportation Decision Process," memorandum from the Federal Highway Administrator and Acting Deputy Urban Mass Transportation Administrator.

——. 1979f. Nondiscrimination on the Bases of Handicap in Federally-Assisted Programs and Activities Receiving or Benefiting from Federal Financial Assistance, *Federal Register*, 44, No. 106, (May 31), pp. 31442–82.

——. (UMTA). 1979g. Urban Initiatives Program; Program Guidlines, *Federal Register*, 44, No. 70 (April 10), pp. 21580–83.

——. (UMTA). 1978. Policy Toward Rail Transit, *Federal Register*, 43, No. 45 (March 7), pp. 9428–30.

——. (FHWA). (April) 1977. *Computer Programs for Urban Transportation Planning– PLANPAC/BACKPAC General Information Manual.* Washington, D.C.: U.S. GPO.

——. 1976a. *Urban System Study.* Washington, D.C.: U.S. DOT.

——. (UMTA). 1976b. Major Urban Mass Transportation Investments, *Federal Register*, 41, No. 185 (September 22), pp. 41512–14.

——. (UMTA and FHWA). 1976c. Transportation for Elderly and Handicapped Persons, *Federal Register*, 41, No. 85 (April 30), pp. 18234–41.

——. (UMTA). 1976d. Charter and School Bus Operations, *Federal Register*, 41, (April 1), pp. 14123–31.

——. (FHWA and UMTA). 1975a. Planning Assistance and Standards, *Federal Register*, 40, No. 181 (September 17), pp. 42976–84.

——. (July) 1975b. *1974 National Transportation Report: Current Performance and Future Prospects.* Washington, D.C.: U.S. GPO.

——. (UMTA). 1975c. Major Urban Mass Transportation Investments, *Federal Register*, 40 (August 1), pp. 32546–47.

—— (FHWA). (May 10) 1974. *Progress Report on Implementation of Process Guidelines.* Washington, D.C.: U.S. DOT.

—— (FHWA). (September 21) 1972a. Policy and Procedure Memorandum 90-4, Process Guidelines (Economic, Social and Environmental Effects on Highway Projects). Washington, D.C.

——. (July) 1972b. *1972 National Transportation Report: Present Status—Future Alternatives.* Washington, D.C.: U.S. GPO.

—— (FHWA). 1970a. *Stewardship Report on Administration of the Federal-Aid Highway Program 1956–1970.* Washington, D.C.: U.S. DOT.

——. (FHWA). (November) 1970b. *Highway Environment Reference Book.* Washington, D.C.: U.S. DOT.

——. (FHWA). (January 14) 1969. Policy and Procedure Memorandum 20-8, Public Hearings and Location Approval. Washington, D.C.

——. (FHW Administration). 1969b. 1968 National Highway Functional Classification Study Manual, Washington, D.C., April.

—— (FHWA). (May 3) 1968. Instructional Memorandum 50-4-68, Operations Plans for "Continuing" Urban Transportation Planning. Washington, D.C.

—— (FHWA). (June 21) 1967a. Policy and Procedure Memorandum 50-9, Urban Transportation Planning. Washington, D.C.

—— (FHWA). (June) 1967b. *Guidelines for Trip Generation Analysis*. Washington, D.C.: U.S. GPO.

—— (FHWA). (August 18) 1967c. Instructional Memorandum 21-13-67, Reserved Bus Lanes. Washington, D.C.

—— and U.S. Department of Housing and Urban Development (HUD). 1974. *Report to the Congress of the United States on Urban Transportation Policies and Activities*. Washington, D.C.: U.S. DOT and HUD.

U.S. Housing and Home Finance Administration and U.S. Department of Commerce. (January) 1965. *Standard Land Use Coding Manual*. Washington, D.C.: U.S. GPO.

Voorhees, Alan M., 1956. A General Theory of Traffic Movement. *1955 Proceedings*. New Haven: Institute of Traffic Engineers.

——. 1955. *A General Theory of Traffic Movement*. The 1955 Past President's Award Paper, Institute of Traffic Engineers, Special Report.

Washington Center for Metropolitan Studies. 1970. *Comprehensive Planning for Metropolitan Development*, prepared for U.S. DOT, UMTA, Washington, D.C.

Weiner, Edward. 1984. "Devolution of the federal role in urban transportation," *J. Adv. Transportation*, 18, No. 2.

——. 1984/5. "Urban transportation planning in the U.S.—An historical overview," in *Transport Reviews*, Part 1 (vol. 4, no. 4, Oct.–Dec. 1984); Part 2 (vol. 5, no. 1, Jan.–Mar. 1985). London: Taylor and Francis.

——. 1983. "Redefinition of roles and responsibilities in U.S. transportation," *Transportation*, Vol. 17. The Hague, The Netherlands: Martinus Nijhoff, pp. 211–24.

——. 1982. "New directions for transportation policy," *J. Amer. Planning Assoc.*, 48, No. 3 (Summer).

——. 1979. "Evolution of urban transportation planning," in *Public Transportation: Planning, Operations, and Management* (Chapter 15), G. Gray and L. Hoel (eds.). Englewood Cliffs, NJ: Prentice-Hall.

——. 1976. "Assessing national urban transportation policy alternatives," in *Transportation Research*, Vol. 10. London: Pergamon Press, pp. 159–78.

——. 1975a. *Workshop 3: The Planner's Role, Research Needs for Evaluating Urban Public Transportation*, Special Report 155. Washington, D.C.: Transportation Research Board, pp. 40–44.

——. (January) 1975b. *Urban Area Results of the 1974 National Transportation Study*. Washington, D.C.: U.S. DOT.

——. 1974. "Urban issues in the 1974 National Transportation Study." Presented at the ASCE/EIC/RTAC Joint Transportation Engineering Meeting, Montreal, Canada, July, 1974.

Wells, John D., Norman J. Asher, Richard P. Brennan, Jane-Ring Crane, Janet D. Kiernan, and Edmund H. Mantell. (June) 1970. *An Analysis of the Financial and Institutional Framework for Urban Transportation Planning and Investment*. Arlington, VA: Institute for Defense Analysis.

Suggestions for Further Reading

Gray, George E. and Lester A. Hoel (eds.). 1979. *Public Transportation: Planning, Operations and Management*. Englewood Cliffs, NJ: Prentice-Hall.

Levinson, Herbert S. and Robert A. Weant (eds.). 1982. *Urban Transportation: Perspectives and Prospects*. Westport, CT: Eno Foundation for Transportation, Inc.

Transportation Research Board. 1984. *Travel Analysis Methods for the 1980s*, Special Report 201. Washington, D.C.: U.S. GPO.

——. 1982. *Urban Transportation Planning in the 1980s*, Special Report 196. Washington, D.C.: U.S. GPO.

U.S. Department of Transportation, Federal Highway Administration. 1979. *America's Highways, 1776–1976, A History of the Federal Aid Program*. Washington, D.C.: U.S. GPO.

Wachs, Martin, 1982. "Symposium: Emerging themes in transportation policy," *J. Amer. Planning Assoc.* 48, No. 3 (Summer).

INDEX

117

ABOUT THE AUTHOR

Edward Weiner has been a Senior Policy Analyst in the Office of the Secretary of the U.S. Department of Transportation since 1970. Mr. Weiner is responsible for urban transportation and highway policy, planning, and legislative issues. Prior to that he was a highway engineer for six years in the Urban Planning Division of the U.S. Federal Highway Administration. He received a B.A. and a B.C.E. from New York University; an M.S.C.E. in Urban Planning from Purdue University; and an M.P.A. from the University of Southern California. He has authored papers on national transportation policy, travel demand forecasting, transportation evaluation, transit needs, financing, and urban transportation planning. He is active on several Transportation Research Board committees and is a Registered Professional Engineer.